BALANCING LITERACY
A BALANCED APPROACH TO READING AND WRITING INSTRUCTION

Written by
Dr. Margaret Allen, Ph.D.

Editor: Carla Hamaguchi
Illustrator: Linda Weller
Cover Illustrator: Reggie Holladay
Designer: Moonhee Pak
Cover Designer: Moonhee Pak
Art Director: Tom Cochrane
Project Director: Carolea Williams

Table of Contents

Dear Teachers,

Over the past decade, we teachers have struggled in our thinking and actions about what is best for young children and the literacy process. We have been a part of a number of pendulum swings. Currently, however, with the broad base of research and with examples from classroom practice, we are closer than ever before to understanding what children need and what teachers can do to meet their needs. We know that we have a nationwide goal that virtually every child will read and write well, that no child will be left behind. This is an admirable goal, for literacy is well recognized as the key to becoming an independent learner in all of the other disciplines.

In my own struggles to meet all children's needs—across grade, socioeconomic, and background levels—I have tried many processes, programs, and activities. Each time the educational pendulum would swing and I tried yet another literacy program, some children inevitably "fell through the instructional cracks." That is, until I understood what a "balanced literacy perspective" is all about. With balanced literacy, I can meet ALL children's needs. In the past, the new "program du jour" would drive the instruction, but with balanced literacy, what we know about what children need and how they learn leads the instruction. From the knowledge base follow processes to meet all children's needs, processes involving whole-group, small-group, and independent work. Teachers select materials and activities that complement the balanced literacy perspective.

Current literacy and brain research tells us that involving different modalities will help children learn new information and retain it. We know that age-appropriate methods can stimulate the development of phonemic awareness, increase the learning of phonics skills, and set children on the path to successful reading and writing. We also know that these same methods can redirect those readers and writers who have fallen by the wayside to get back on the path to success.

For these reasons, I gladly share my thinking and understanding of a balanced literacy perspective with you, my fellow educators. I hope you find these ideas, processes, and activities beneficial in meeting the needs of ALL of YOUR children!

Sincerely,
Dr. Margaret Allen, Ph.D. (Dr. Maggie)

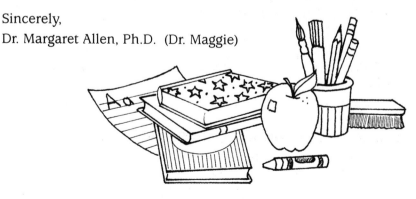

Introduction

What are the components of a balanced literacy program? How do you incorporate all of them into your school day? *Balancing Literacy K–2* answers these questions and more.

This comprehensive resource guide is divided into seven main sections. The first section, Creating a Balanced Literacy Program, describes the classroom environment and provides sample schedules that show how to implement all the components. The next three sections describe the literacy processes: phonemic awareness, phonics, and spelling; writing; and reading. Although these processes are separated into sections, they should not be taught separately. These processes overlap. For example, a shared writing activity produces a chart that children first read during a whole-group lesson and use later at a writing literacy center to practice phonics skills.

The fifth section, Literacy Centers, presents ideas for creating literacy areas in your classroom. Children can work independently in these areas while you are working with small groups of children (e.g., guided reading). Many of the items that you will place in your centers will come from whole-group activities (e.g., shared or modeled writing).

The Assessment section provides a brief description of various assessment methods and reproducible assessment forms. The last section addresses the needs of English-language learners and provides several teaching strategies and game ideas to aid their learning process.

After reading through this resource, decide what works for your children and best meets their needs, and implement those ideas. Remember, the key to making everything fit is to overlap the literacy processes.

There has been extensive research on early literacy and the ways children learn best. This "literate schoolhouse" is a visual to help you better understand the findings of many researchers. The schoolhouse is an exciting place where literacy is the cornerstone of every process; where teachers address children's basic literacy needs in meaningful ways; and where instruction, repetition, and mastery of skills are based on multimodal, brain-based experiences.

Building Literacy

Oral Language

The foundation for learning is oral language. This includes everything the child has heard, read, and talked about up to the moment, including thoughts and feelings and all sensory experiences. Both receptive language (the ability to hear and understand) and expressive language (the ability to speak and express thoughts) are the foundation for reading and writing. Children with well-developed oral language will

- more easily engage in discussions with books

- feel more self-confident as beginning readers and writers

- develop an understanding of sounds in words (phonemic awareness)

- more readily recognize concepts about print and the alphabet

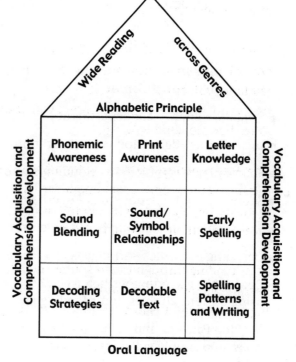

Wide Reading across Genres

The overarching "ceiling" of this literate schoolhouse is a range of literature from many genres in multiple formats. It includes

- Shared Reading—reading of patterned, predictable books as part of a whole-class reading experience

- Informative Reading—reading information books to gain new vocabulary and concepts, as well as reading written messages and directions

- Guided Reading—small-group work in which the teacher works with each group at its individual reading level with patterned predictable books

- Independent Reading—children reading independently to practice what they are learning

- Modeled Reading—time during which the teacher would read aloud at everyone's higher "listening level" so that he or she could introduce and discuss more sophisticated syntax patterns, vocabulary, and concepts

Vocabulary Acquisition and Comprehension Development

The "walls" of vocabulary acquisition and comprehension development are built strong to endure. Children unlock the nine individual "rooms" in the schoolhouse as they develop the alphabetic principle—the ability to independently unlock the code of how sound maps into symbol so that the child can accurately and quickly "lift the print off the page." Individual rooms consist of the following:

- Phonemic Awareness—the understanding that a word consists of individual sounds in a specific order

- Print Awareness—concepts about print

- Letter Knowledge—alphabet recognition

- Sound Blending—multiple blending strategies

- Sound/Symbol Relationships—synthetic and analytic phonics

- Early Spelling—encoding based on current level of sound/symbol understanding

- Decoding Strategies—strategies to successfully lift print off the page

- Decodable Text—text written to practice sight words and decodable words using current phonics and decoding skills

- Spelling Patterns and Writing—the basic vowel patterns, structural analysis skills, and simple syllabication strategies necessary to decode to read and encode to write

To help children obtain the "keys" to these nine rooms, teach them how to listen for sounds and the patterns they make, look at print and patterns of print, and then extend that information and apply it to words with multiple syllables.

Thus, children use this information to decode to read and to encode to spell and write. The two processes of reading and writing are reciprocal and must be modeled as such so that children make the connection and understand WHY they are learning the individual skills you present to them.

What are the components of a balanced literacy program? The following pages describe each component and explain how it fits into a balanced literacy program.

Shared Reading: Teacher and children read enlarged text together

- Builds a "community" of readers

- Promotes reading strategies

- Increases awareness of concepts of print

- Builds sight word vocabulary

- Develops fluency

- Increases comprehension

- Expands children's vocabulary

Modeled Reading (The Read-Aloud): Teacher reads aloud selections to children

- Provides a model of reading fluency with expression

- Develops story comprehension

- Enriches concept and vocabulary development

- Provides opportunity to hear sophisticated story syntax

- Encourages prediction

- Fosters enthusiasm for reading

Guided Reading: Teacher selects appropriate text for a small group of children who are similar in strengths and needs to provide instruction that targets specific reading strategies

- Promotes student use of a variety of reading strategies

- Develops comprehension

- Encourages independent reading

- Strengthens thinking skills

- Allows teacher to work with individual groups of children on specific reading skills

- Builds sight word vocabulary

Independent Reading: Children read independently

- Extends reading fluency
- Develops automaticity with word recognition
- Supports writing development
- Promotes reading for enjoyment and information
- Fosters self-confidence as children read familiar and new text

Modeled and Shared Writing: Teacher and children collaborate to generate text, but the teacher writes the text

- Develops concepts about print
- Develops writing strategies
- Supports reading of text
- Provides a model for various writing styles
- Produces text that children can read independently

Interactive Writing: Using a "shared pen" technique, teacher and children together create text in which children do some of the writing

- Provides authentic opportunity for writing
- Models the use of phonics skills for writing
- Increases spelling knowledge
- Provides written language resources for future classroom use

Guided Writing: Teacher works with individual or small groups of children who are similar in strengths and needs to provide instruction through mini-lessons

- Provides powerful model for organization and brainstorming of ideas
- Guides children through the writing process

Independent Writing: Children write independently

- Develops an understanding of multiple uses of writing
- Strengthens text sequence
- Supports reading development
- Supports spelling development
- Develops writing strategies

Teaching Tools

Use this list of helpful supplies and hints to enhance children's learning.

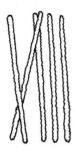

Wikki Stix®
Have children use them to highlight words, letters, or punctuation on charts.

Die Cuts
Have children use them to generate writing ideas. Or, write words on die cuts, and cut the words into separate pieces to make phonics puzzles.

Craft Sticks
Decorate them to make fun reading pointers.

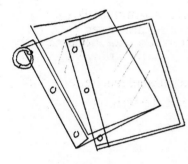

Plastic Sleeves
Store overhead transparencies in plastic sleeves, and place them at learning centers.

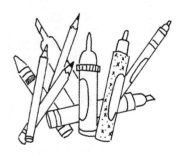

Correction Tape
Use pieces of white correction tape to cover writing mistakes on charts during interactive writing.

Paint Sticks
Write words or draw pictures on index cards to make word or picture cards. Place Velcro® on the back of each word or picture card. Place the opposing pieces of Velcro on several paint sticks. Invite children to attach a card to a stick, walk around the room with the stick, and look for that word in books or on charts.

Writing Materials
Invite children to use crayons, pens, markers, puffy paint, glitter glue, and colored pencils during group and independent writing activities. These art materials motivate children to participate.

Creating a Balanced Literacy Program

You may be wondering how to implement all of the components of a balanced literacy program into your classroom schedule. Although there is no single approach that works for everyone, the following pages provide a tour of a balanced literacy classroom, including a description of what it might look like, a list of suggested materials, and sample schedules. The two sample schedules include Reader's and Writer's Workshop. These two organizational components are devoted to numerous reading and writing processes. They are organized in a single block of instructional time so that they flow from one to the other, providing an optimal way to preview and review skills from both components.

A balanced literacy program involves numerous processes to strengthen reading, writing, and spelling. Do not expect to introduce all of them simultaneously. Take time to gradually introduce and model each new process. Start with whole-group processes to get to know your children and their attitudes and aptitudes. Then, add small-group, partner, and individual activities and processes based on your informal assessments and observations. By making sure your children understand each process and procedure, you will ensure that your result will be an efficient and effective balanced literacy program.

Guided Reading
Interactive Writing
Phonics
Literacy Centers
Assessment

The first step to creating a balanced literacy program is to establish your classroom environment. The following is a suggested list of things to include in your classroom:

Creating the Classroom Environment

- a large open area for whole-group reading, meetings, story dramatizations, and music and movement activities

- areas for small-group, partner, and independent work

- environmental and functional print with directions and labels posted

- stories, messages, lists, class-made books, and other written materials produced by children

- a classroom library with books for independent and instructional reading organized for quick selection by genre, reading level, or theme

- reading materials, including children's literature, predictable books, decodable books, trade books, newspapers, student-made books, content-related books, and children's magazines

- poems, songs, and charts and sentence strips for pocket chart use

- read-the-room pointers and highlighters

- writing materials that are easily available for student use

- computers, educational software, reference materials, and word wall(s)

- portfolios and authentic assessment tools

- literacy centers organized in areas: Reading, Writing and Illustrating, Spelling and Word Work, and Listening Post

- developmental centers/project materials for science, math, and social studies, including supportive fiction and nonfiction books

- "sense of community" but one in which diversity and individualism are accepted and appreciated, where labels and artifacts from various cultures/languages are present

What Does a Balanced Literacy Room Look Like?

When you look into a balanced literacy classroom, you may see the following:

- children participating in shared and interactive reading and writing experiences

- children involved in comprehension-building activities

- teacher providing ongoing informal and formal assessment to monitor student progress

- teacher modifying instruction based on children's needs

- children discussing stories and working with peers

- teacher conferencing with children to discuss their work

- teacher using a variety of methods and materials (such as music, art, and hands-on manipulatives) to teach reading and writing

- children working in whole-group, small-group, and individual settings

Setting Up Your Classroom

This diagram shows a suggested way to arrange your classroom furniture.

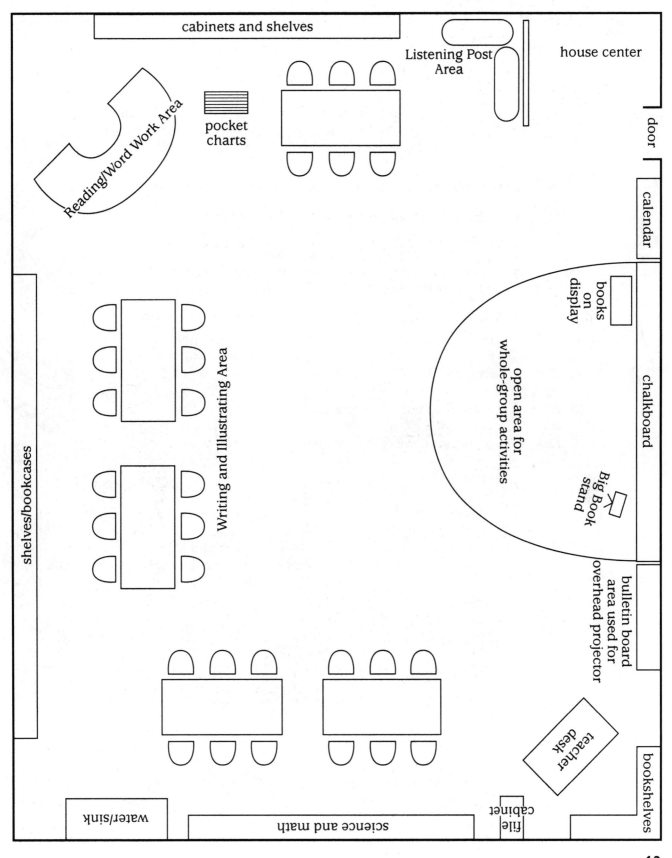

A Sample Daily Schedule for Full-Day Programs

8:00–8:15	Book Browsing/Independent Reading Time (S.S.R.)
8:15–8:40	Morning Meeting, Calendar, Morning Message, Daily News

8:40–10:10	Reader's Workshop
	  Shared Reading—Whole Class
	  Guided Reading/Small-Group Work
	  Literacy Centers
	  Shared Reading and Guided Reading Follow-up Activities
	  Read-Aloud

10:10–10:25	Recess

10:25–11:05	Writer's Workshop
	  Journal Writing
	  Teacher-Modeled Mini-lessons
	  Handwriting
	  Guided Writing
	  Process Writing

11:05–11:30	Developmental Center Time (Gr. K–1); Project Time (Gr. 2)
11:30–12:00	Lunch
12:00–12:15	Phonemic Awareness and Word Work
12:15–12:45	Art, Music, Library, or Computer Lab
12:45–1:15	Math
1:15–1:45	Physical Education
1:45–2:15	Theme Time (Social Studies, Science, Health and Safety) Structure Writing/Content Writing (in response to new content learned)
2:15–2:25	Read-Aloud Time (teacher reads to class)
2:25–2:50	Sharing and Wrap Up Time (Gr. K) Writing in "My Forever Journal" Independent Reading Time or Story Circles (Gr.1–2)
2:50–3:00	Cleanup
3:00	Dismissal

A Sample Daily Schedule for Half-Day Programs

8:00–8:25	Developmental Center Time
8:25–8:45	Morning Meeting, Calendar, Morning Message, Daily News
8:45–9:05	Writer's Workshop 　　　　Journal Writing 　　　　Teacher-Modeled Mini-lessons 　　　　Independent Writing 　　　　Handwriting
9:05–10:05	Reader's Workshop 　　　　Shared Reading—Whole Class 　　　　Small-Group Work/Guided Reading 　　　　Reading Follow-up Activities 　　　　Literacy Centers 　　　　Read-Aloud
10:05–10:25	Recess/Physical Education
10:25–10:45	Math
10:45–11:05	Theme Time (Science, Social Studies, Health and Safety)
11:05–11:30	Writing in "My Forever Journal" Cleanup
11:30	Dismissal

Phonemic Awareness, Phonics, and Spelling

Phonemic awareness is the understanding that words are made up of a series of specific sounds. Phonics is the study of how those sounds map into symbols. Spelling is the orthography of words. The three are all related processes. Children need to be able to hear sounds and patterns of sounds in words; they need to recognize print and patterns of print in words; and they need to know how those patterns fit together to make single and polysyllabic words. Once they understand these processes, they will be able to decode to read words and encode to spell and write words. Have children use their phonics skills on a daily basis. Ask children to write words letter by letter or chunk by chunk as they spell them or during reading when they decode them letter by letter or chunk by chunk.

Children need explicit instruction that is based on a developmentally appropriate scope and sequence and tied to a meaningful text (e.g., song, poem, story) in order to understand how the English language works. Have children use word walls and other high-frequency word activities to practice irregular words. Frequently engage children in activities that include phonics patterns and sight words so they can recognize them automatically when they read and retrieve them quickly from their mind when they spell.

As you organize your thinking and materials to develop a sound phonics and spelling program, review the following primary scope and sequence for introduction of sound, letter, and word recognition components.

Scope and Sequence

Oral Language Development
>   Receptive (what a child can hear and understand)
>   Expressive (how well a child can use verbal language)

Sound Awareness
>   Sound Recognition of the Environment
>   Onomatopoeia
>   Timbre of Voices and Instruments

Phonological Awareness/Phonemic Awareness
>   Hearing (includes words, rhyme, syllables, alliteration, onset/rime, segmentation of sounds, blending sounds, substitution of sounds)

Print Awareness
>   Concepts about Print (directionality, punctuation, capitalization)
>   Environmental Print (store and product logos)
>   Labels (objects in room)
>   Names (class members' names, family names, common words)
>   Sight Words (high-frequency and irregular words)
>   Phonics (single letter/sound combinations and chunks)
>   Synthetic Phonics (consonants, vowels, blends, digraphs)
>   Analytic Phonics (word families or phonograms)
>   Vowel Patterns
>> Closed-vowel pattern *(cat)*
>> Open-vowel pattern *(go)*
>> Silent *e* pattern *(like)*
>> Vowel-team pattern
>>> digraphs *(rain)*
>>> diphthongs *(foil)*
>> *R*-controlled pattern *(bird)*
>> Consonant + *le* pattern *(apple)*

Practice with Decodable Text (early readers)

Structural Analysis
>   Root Words with Affixes (prefixes and suffixes)
>   Contractions
>   Compound Words

Syllabication

Word Study/Word Origin (roots and their meanings)

Phonemic Awareness

For children to develop phonemic awareness (the awareness that each word is made up of specific sounds and the ability to "play" with sounds of language) they need repeated opportunities to listen to and play with language. Use the following teaching strategies and activities to help children develop phonemic awareness.

Letter/Word Awareness activities help children quickly recognize specific letters and words and develop their automaticity and fluency with letter and word recognition. Research supports the need for children to master basic skills at the automaticity level so they can focus on their comprehension of what they read.

Blending sounds is the core of reading words, so it is helpful for children to develop blending developmentally. Teach children to blend the onset or beginning sound to the rime or phonogram (e.g., *c* with *-at,* or *b* with *-ed*). Then, teach children to blend by having them segment each sound in the word and then put the sounds together.

Phonemic Awareness Activities

Body Beats

Ask children to choose a way to make sounds with their body (body percussion) such as clapping their hands or tapping their tummy. Recite a familiar rhyme, and have children use body percussion to keep the beat.

Pom-Pom Syllables

Write each child's name on a cardboard strip. Glue a small pom-pom under each syllable. Give children their name strip. Have children touch each pom-pom as they read their name. Remind them that each time they touch a different pom-pom they are saying a syllable in their name. Invite children to read and count the syllables in their classmates' names.

Stomping Syllables

Write the lyrics to "Hot Cross Buns" on a piece of chart paper, or copy the Hot Cross Buns reproducible (page 20) on an overhead transparency. Sing the song with the class. When children are familiar with the song, have them sing the song and stomp their feet on each syllable. Challenge children by having them stomp every time they sing a single-syllable word and clap each time they sing a two-syllable word.

Hot Cross Buns

Hot cross buns.
Hot cross buns.
One a penny,
Two a penny,
Hot cross buns.

Balancing Literacy • K–2 © 2002 Creative Teaching Press

Letter/Word Awareness Activities

Feed the Monster

Make a monster mask with eyeholes and a large hole for the mouth. Place the mask on an overhead projector. Make a set of letter cards or sight word cards on an overhead transparency. Turn out the lights in the classroom, and place a row of letter or sight word cards on the projector. Pretend the "monster" is saying *Feed me a (letter or sight word)*. Slowly move the letter or sight word card through the monster's cutout mouth and under the opaque part of the mask. It should look like the monster is eating the letter or word. Extend the activity by letting students "feed" the monster.

Rolling Letters

Write large capital letters on individual paper plates. Give each child a plate. Call out a letter, and have the child with that letter plate hold it up and spin it around. As the child spins the plate, have the class sing the following to the tune of "The Farmer in the Dell":

> The _____ is rolling around.
> The _____ is rolling around.
> As soon as the letter _____ stops,
> Name something that starts with its sound.

Swat the Letter

Obtain a flyswatter and a pair of tweezers. Copy and cut apart a set of Letter Cards (pages 22–24). Place the cards on a table, or pin them to a wall. Call out a letter, and invite a child to use the flyswatter to swat the correct card and then pick up the card with the tweezers. Then, challenge the child to spell a word that begins with the letter.

Letter Cards

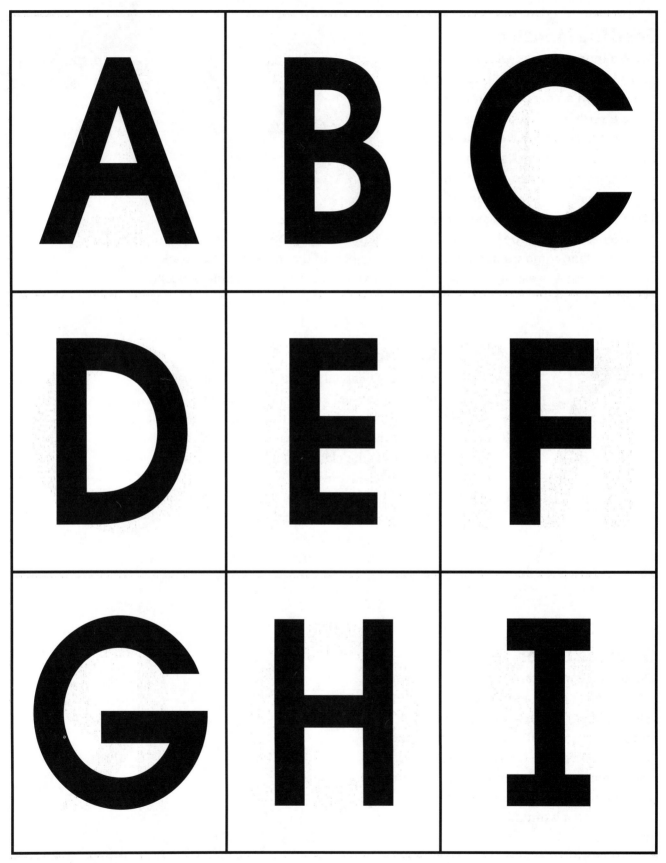

Phonemic Awareness, Phonics, and Spelling

Balancing Literacy • K–2 © 2002 Creative Teaching Press

Letter Cards

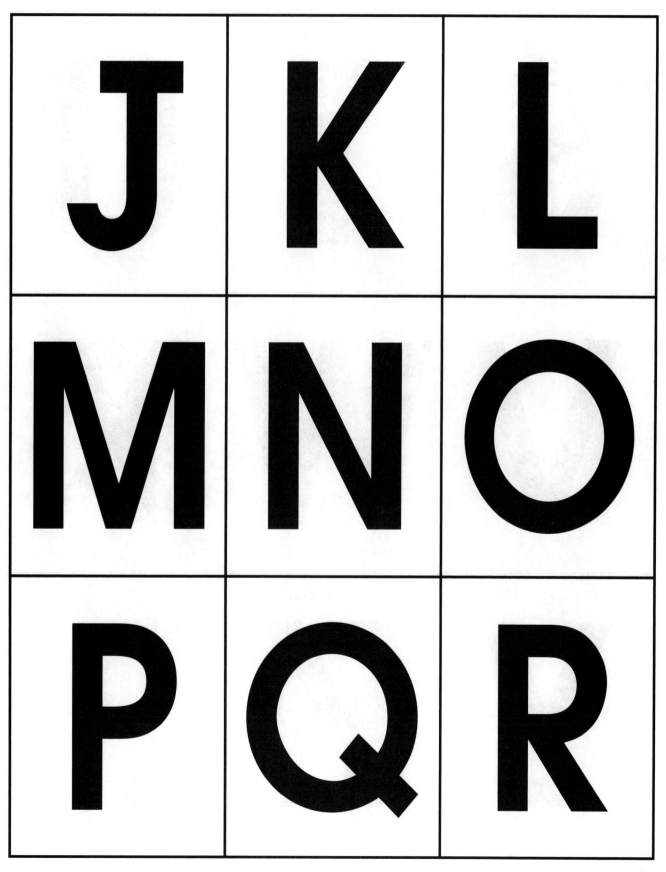

Phonemic Awareness, Phonics, and Spelling

Letter Cards

Balancing Literacy • K–2 © 2002 Creative Teaching Press

Blending Activities

Blending Slide

Draw a large slide on a piece of chart paper. Copy and cut apart a set of Letter Cards (pages 22–24). Choose a simple word. Use nonpermanent tape to attach the corresponding letter cards to the slide. Move the first letter card down the slide, and say its sound. Then, slide the second letter card into the first letter, and blend the sounds together. Continue this process to blend the sounds and read the whole word. This method,

known as successive blending, is effective for children who have difficulty segmenting letters and blending their sounds. Choose another word, and invite volunteers to move the cards and blend the sounds to say the word.

Letter Chain

Choose a word. Write each letter on a separate sticky note. Have volunteers stand in front of the class and link together large paper clips to make a chain. Stick each sticky note to a paper clip in the center of the chain. Point out that just as the paper clips link together to form a chain, the letters link together to form a word. Have children blend the sounds to read the word. Repeat the activity with other words.

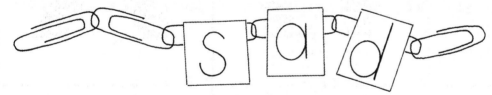

Link to Blend

Copy and cut apart a set of Letter Cards (pages 22–24). Choose a word. Have volunteers stand in front of the class and hold the corresponding letter cards. Ask each child to say the sound his or her letter makes. Then, have the first child say the sound, hold it, and link arms with the second child. Have the second child quickly say his or her sound and link arms with the third child, who quickly says his or her letter's sound. In this way, children quickly link or blend together the three sounds to say the word.

Phonics

Children are ready for sound/letter pairing or phonics when they have phonemic awareness, have some letter awareness, and can recognize a core of consonants. Use jingles, chants, and stories to teach phonics patterns to children. Pictures and dramatization increase recall, especially for English-language learners and dyslexic children. Avoid a rule-laden program in which children memorize and then recall rules on demand to facilitate word recognition. The human brain functions as a pattern detector rather than as a rule memorizer and implementer.

Phonics work should begin with basic elements, such as simple sound/letter matching, and move to more complex and subtle elements, such as vowel patterns and two-syllable words. Although more than one complex element, such as multiple letter combinations that represent a long vowel sound (e.g., *a-e, ai, ay*), may be a focus skill, teach only one sound/letter pairing at a time. Work with the skill until children begin to internalize it, and then teach other sound/letter pairings that make the same sound. For example, teach *a-e*, and then introduce *ai* and then *ay* when teaching the long *a* sound.

Basic vowel patterns include the following:

- the closed-vowel pattern (as in *cat, bed,* and *pig*)

- the long-vowel pattern in which the vowel ends the word (as in *me, hi,* and *go*)

- the silent *e* long-vowel pattern (as in *make, bite,* and *note*)

- the vowel-digraph pattern ("when two vowels go out walking, the first one does the talking" as in *boat* and *rain*)

- the vowel-diphthong pattern (as in *cow, toy,* and *oil*)

- the *r*-controlled pattern (as in *car, first,* and *turn*)

- the consonant *-le* pattern (as in *purple* and *apple*)

Encourage children to write to make use of their phonics skills. Children reveal their level of phonics understanding when they invent spellings of words based on their understanding of how language works. (Be sure children spell sight words conventionally once they learn them.) As children move up the developmental ladder, their knowledge of phonics rises, and they move closer to using conventional spellings. If forced to use conventional spelling too quickly, children may not develop the underlying knowledge of how language works and must rely on their memory alone when writing.

Phonics Activities

Word Sorts

Draw a picture of a tree, and write *tree* on it. Ask children to tell you a word that rhymes with *tree*. Encourage children to include non-sense words (e.g., *ree*). Write each response on a separate index card. Explain to children that although the words rhyme, they are spelled differently and have different vowel patterns. Ask them to tell you what vowel patterns make the *ee* sound (i.e., *ey, e, ea*). Place the word cards and copies of the My Word Sort reproducible (page 28) in the Spelling and Word Work Area (see page 111). Invite children to first separate the real words from the nonsense words. Ask them to write the two sets of words on the top half of their reproducible. Then, have them sort the word cards according to the vowel patterns. Then, have them write each vowel pattern at the top of a separate column under "Category Sort" on their reproducible. Ask children to write each word in the correct column.

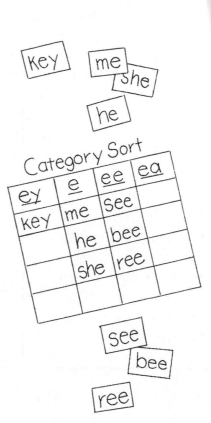

Word Detectives

Write *by, my, sly, fry,* and *try* on the left side of a two-column chart. Write *very, scary, angry,* and *slowly* on the right side. Have volunteers use a marker to highlight the last letter in each word. Ask children what they notice about these words. Have children read aloud the left column of words. Ask *In each word, what sound does **y** at the end make?* Do the same with the right column. Reread the words in the left column, and clap the syllables. Ask *Which column has one-syllable words? Which column has two-syllable words? What do we notice in these two columns about the **y** sound?* Lead children to observe that the *y* ending in one-syllable words makes a long *i* sound, while the same ending in two-syllable words makes a long *e* sound.

Name _____   Date _____

My Word Sort

Real Words	Nonsense Words

Category Sort

_____	_____	_____	_____

Phonemic Awareness, Phonics, and Spelling

Balancing Literacy • K–2 © 2002 Creative Teaching Press

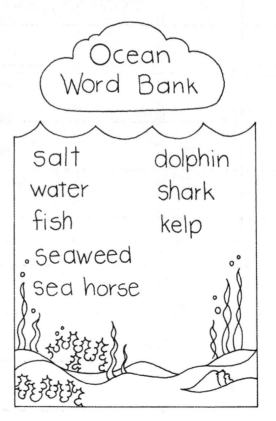

Use these fun word wall ideas to create meaningful word walls and word work activities to help children improve their spelling. The ideas are listed in a developmental progression. Choose which type of word wall best fits your children's needs. Remember to change word walls throughout the school year. Remove words students have mastered, and add new words to your walls.

● Names and Common Words

Include the names of each child in the class and common objects and animals. Include a simple drawing next to each word to provide visual clues for emergent readers. Place a photograph of each child next to his or her name.

● High-Frequency Words

See page 30 for a list of 100 frequently used words. These are words that children cannot learn through the use of pictures. Children must recognize these words before they can read with confidence.

● Theme Word Banks

Create portable word banks to complement a unit of study. For example, decorate poster board and write a list of ocean-related words for an ocean unit.

● Vowel Patterns and Vowel Chunks

Include word families (e.g., *-at, -atch, -ight*) or vowel patterns (e.g., *ai* in *rain, faint, painter*). See page 31 for a list of basic rimes.

● Homophones

Include homophones that children often misuse. For example, children write *I have a blew car* rather than *I have a blue car*. See page 32 for a list of homophones.

● Root Words

Include root words with endings (e.g., *-s, -ed, -ing, -er*) or root words that present patterns of sound, print, and meaning (e.g., *port—deport, import, report, export*). See page 33 for a list of prefixes and suffixes.

High-Frequency Words

a	go	more	then
about	good	my	there
all	great	no	these
an	had	not	they
and	has	now	this
are	have	of	time
as	he	off	to
at	her	on	too
be	here	one	two
because	him	only	up
been	his	or	use
but	how	other	very
by	I	out	was
can	if	over	way
come	in	people	we
could	into	said	were
day	is	see	what
do	it	she	when
does	like	should	which
down	look	so	who
each	made	some	will
first	make	than	with
for	many	the	word
from	may	their	would
get	me	them	you

Balancing Literacy • K–2 © 2002 Creative Teaching Press

Basic Rimes

Nearly 500 primary-grade words can be derived from the following set of 37 rimes.

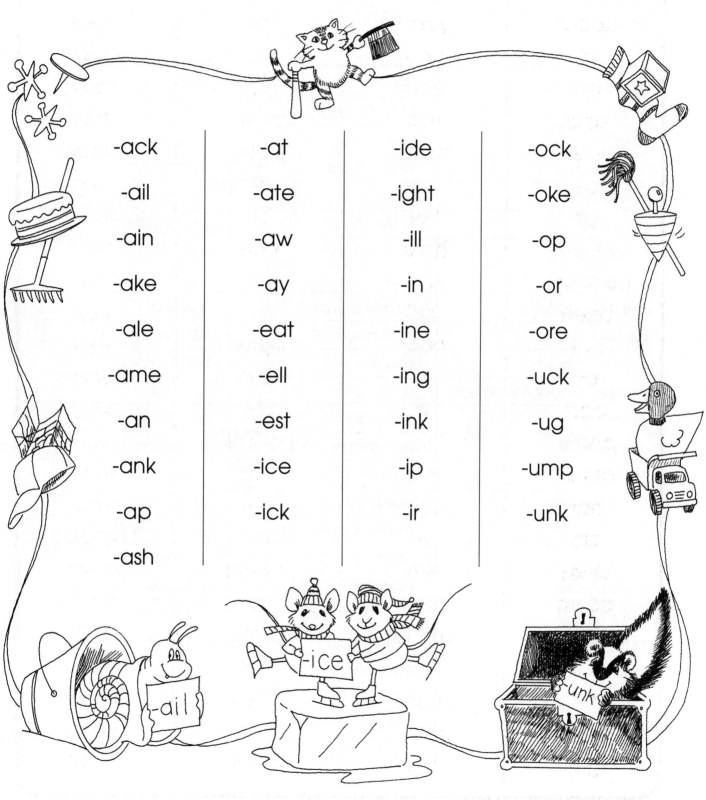

-ack	-at	-ide	-ock
-ail	-ate	-ight	-oke
-ain	-aw	-ill	-op
-ake	-ay	-in	-or
-ale	-eat	-ine	-ore
-ame	-ell	-ing	-uck
-an	-est	-ink	-ug
-ank	-ice	-ip	-ump
-ap	-ick	-ir	-unk
-ash			

Homophones

Homophones are words that sound the same but have different spellings or meanings. This is a list of the most common homophones.

aloud/allowed	I/eye	road/rode
ate/eight	knead/need	role/roll
bear/bare	knew/new	sail/sale
beat/beet	knight/night	scene/seen
billed/build	know/no	sea/see
blew/blue	knows/nose	sew/so/sow
bored/board	made/maid	sighed/side
brake/break	mail/male	sight/site/cite
capital/capitol	new/knew/gnu	stair/stare
cell/sell	not/knot	steak/stake
cent/sent/scent	oh/owe	straight/strait
compliment/complement	one/won	tale/tail
creak/creek	pail/pale	they're/there/their
dear/deer	pain/pane	threw/through
die/dye	pair/pear/pare	to/too/two
do/due/dew	past/passed	tow/toe
fare/fair	patients/patience	wade/weighed
flour/flower	pause/paws	wait/weight
for/four/fore	peak/peek	waste/waist
hair/hare	piece/peace	week/weak
hay/hey	plain/plane	which/witch
heal/heel/he'll	presents/presence	whole/hole
hear/here	principle/principal	would/wood
hole/whole	raise/rays/raze	wring/ring
horse/hoarse	read/red	
hour/our	right/write/rite	

Prefixes and Suffixes

A prefix is a letter group added before a base word or root word to add to or change the meaning of the word.

Most Common Prefixes

Prefix	Meaning	Example
anti-	against	antiwar
de-	opposite	degrade
dis-	opposite	dishonest
en-, em-	cause to	enlighten
fore-	before	forethought
in-, im-, ir-, ill-	not	irresponsible
in-, im-	in or into	include, impact
inter-	between, among	interaction
mid-	middle	midsize
mis-	wrongly	misguided
non-	not	nonsense
over-	too much	overstatement
pre-	before	preview
re-	again	replace
semi-	half	semicircle
sub-	under	submarine
super-	above	supernatural
trans-	across	transatlantic
un-	not, opposite of	unbelievable

A suffix is a letter group added after a base word or root word to add to or change the meaning of the word.

Most Common Suffixes

Suffix	Meaning	Suffix	Meaning
-al, -ial	having characteristics of	-ion, -tion, -ation, -ition	act, process
-ed	verb form/past tense	-ity, -ty	state of
-en	made of	-ive, -ative, -itive	adjective form of the noun
-er, -or	person connected with	-less	without
-er	comparative form	-ly	having characteristics of
-est	comparative form	-ment	action or process
-ful	full of	-ness	state of, condition of
-ible, -able	can be done	-ous, -eous, -ious	possessing the qualities of
-ic	having characteristics of	-s, -es	plural form
-ing	verb form/present participle	-y	characterized by

Phonemic Awareness, Phonics, and Spelling

Balancing Literacy • K–2 © 2002 Creative Teaching Press

Writing

Writing is a developmental process that children become more proficient at over time and with practice. Children need to write every day from the first day of school to the last! Children can write lists, notes, stories, poems, and songs; create labels for drawings, art projects and block constructions; and write letters to family members during center time. Children can also make name placards for creative dramatics, create menus, and take restaurant food orders during center time.

To give children all they need to launch into the writing process, model good writing through interactive writing lessons, Morning Message, and daily news and provide authentic writing purposes and opportunities to write on a daily basis. Encourage children to write independently in journals, create stories, and learn the writing process to help them edit and revise their writing.

Children develop their writing skills at various rates. See the Developmental Stages of Writing chart on page 35 to determine which stage each child is at (based on his or her writing characteristics). Give children appropriate activities to meet their needs. See pages 36–42 for suggested writing activities for each developmental stage.

Use the numerous writing formats in this section to provide children with authentic writing purposes and ways to communicate their ideas. These formats include modeled and shared writing, interactive and guided writing, independent writing, process writing, and journal writing.

Developmental Stages of Writing

The following lists describe the characteristics and needs of children at each developmental stage of writing. Use the activities on pages 36–42 to help meet the needs of your writers.

Stage	Characteristics	Needs
Emergent Writer	• Draw pictures to write stories • Use scribbles, symbol writing, or letter strings in early writing attempts • Understand that talk can be written down, but may not understand how the process works • Begin to use left-to-right directional movement • Often "tell" their writing to others to "read" it • Begin to develop phonemic awareness and letter recognition skills, and begin to use those skills to invent spellings, especially with consonants • Begin to participate in frame writing, using common syntax patterns or frames for their writing • Begin to choose writing topics	• Many opportunities to hear literature from all genres read to develop writing models and structures • Opportunities to participate in language experience as teacher writes down a child's talk (teacher as scribe) • Daily opportunities to hear songs, poems, and chants as models for writing • Numerous whole- and small-group modeled and shared writing opportunities • Daily opportunities to self-select topics, write, and share writing • Instruction on phonemic awareness and letter recognition skills • Variety of writing instruments and paper, including lined and unlined paper
Developing Writer	• Use invented spelling approximations in their writing, but over time begin to move toward conventional spelling • Use initial, final, and other consonants more accurately than vowels (vowels are often incorrect or missing) • Spell many high-frequency words correctly • Often use familiar patterns or book models as writing frames • May write and title a simple story that includes a beginning, middle, ending and some simple dialogue • Begin to edit own writing and to use resources to correct invented spelling approximations • May begin to establish a personal style of writing	• Many opportunities to hear literature from all genres read to use as writing models • Daily opportunities to self-select topics, write, and share writing • Numerous whole- and small-group modeled, shared, and interactive writing experiences • Instruction and modeling in the writing process to be able to participate in the complete process with assistance • Instruction and modeling in using phonics skills, vowel pattern knowledge, and structural analysis to be able to write more words conventionally
Fluent Writer	• Understand story structure, and use that information to write stories with a well-defined beginning, middle, and ending • Read to add information to their writing • Demonstrate subject knowledge, and develop the subject or theme with details • Write in a variety of genres • Understand phonics skills, structural analysis, and syllabication, and use that information to write most words conventionally, use resources for words that are unfamiliar or words of which they are unsure • Make verb tenses agree throughout writing • Use conventions of writing—write in paragraphs with correct punctuation • Initiate self-revision and editing to demonstrate personal concern for quality writing	• Opportunities to hear teacher read aloud from all genres to develop writing models, including topic and character development, story structure, and syntax and vocabulary usage • Daily opportunities to self-select topics, write, use the entire writing process, and share writing with peers • Numerous opportunities to conference with peers and with teacher to discuss writing strategies and use of dialogue and to complete the editing process • Instruction and modeling on how to revise their writing for a particular audience of readers and to meet those readers' needs

Emergent Writing Activities

My Magic Word

Create a word bank that consists of
words based on a category of study
(e.g., toys, family members, pets,
household items). Give each child a
white crayon and a white piece of
paper. Ask each child to select a word
from the word bank and write it on
his or her paper. (Of course, it will not
show.) Ask a volunteer to describe his
or her "magic word" to the class with-

out saying the word. Invite the rest of the class to guess what the word is.
Demonstrate how to use a soft lead pencil to shade across the paper until the
word can be seen. Invite the volunteer to rub the pencil across his or her paper
to reveal the word. Have children look for the matching word on the word bank
and read the magic word. Continue the activity with other volunteers.

Pass the Story, Please

Copy the Pass the Story, Please reproducible (page 37) on an overhead transparency. Use the transparency to model your writing. Use a simple story plot
about a class of children and their daily events. Have the class sit in a circle. Tell
children that they are going to take turns telling the story by "passing" it around
the circle as you write their responses on the transparency. Start the story by filling in the first blank of the reproducible (e.g., *One day, at Olmstead School*). Then,
pause to let a child suggest a name for the next blank. Write the name on the
transparency. Pass the responsibility for adding on to the story to the next child
and so on as you continue reading and writing the story on the transparency.
After children are familiar with this process, invite them to follow the "pass the
story" format to create original class stories.

Pass the Story, Please

One day, at _____ School, some children named

_____, _____, and _____

were working on _____.

The _____ rang, and all of the children lined up at the

_____ to go outside to _____.

Everyone played _____ together and had a

lot of _____. When recess was over, it was time to go

back _____. The children went inside to get a

drink of _____ and to wash their _____.

Back in the classroom, the children started to _____ a

good story about _____. Then it was

snack time. The children ate _____ and then

cleaned up to go _____.

It was such a nice day that the teacher said, "_____

_____." All of the children smiled!

Developing Writing Activities

Story Chain

Distribute five different colored sentence strips to five children. Read a story to the five children, and have each child retell part of the story—the introduction, three main events in the middle of the story, and the ending. After children retell the story, have them write their portion of their story on their "link" (sentence strip). Invite children to read aloud their link, and then staple together the ends of the sentence strips to create a "story chain."

Change It!

Sing the rhyme "One, Two, Buckle My Shoe" with the class. Point out the rhyming words. Write the number words on a piece of chart paper. Ask children to brainstorm words that rhyme with each number word (e.g., *one—sun, fun*). Give each child a One, Two, Rewrite for You reproducible (page 39). Have children write words that rhyme with each number word at the top of their paper. Ask them to use words from their list to create an innovation of the familiar rhyme. For example, a child could write *Ten, nine,/Get in line.*

As an extension, sing another familiar song, such as "Down by the Bay" (see page 82), with the class. Write each line of the song on a separate sentence strip, and place the strips in a pocket chart. Call attention to the structure of each line. Ask children to brainstorm new pairs of rhyming words. Write each word on a separate index card. Invite children to place the word cards in the pocket chart to create an innovation. For example, a child could change *Did you ever see a **fly** wearing a **tie**?* to *Did you ever see a **cat** wearing a **hat**?* Invite children to sing the new song and then copy and illustrate it.

Down by the Bay

Did you ever see a [ ] cat

wearing [ ] a [ ] hat

Down by the bay?

Name _____   Date _____

One, Two, Rewrite for You

One	Three	Five	Seven	Nine
_____	_____	_____	_____	_____
_____	_____	_____	_____	_____
_____	_____	_____	_____	_____
_____	_____	_____	_____	_____

My Poem

Title_____

Ten, nine,

_____.

Eight, seven,

_____.

Six, five,

_____.

Four, three,

_____.

Two, one,

_____.

Balancing Literacy • K–2 © 2002 Creative Teaching Press

Fluent Writing Activities

Rhyme to Story

Display a copy of a familiar nursery rhyme such as "Jack and Jill," "Humpty Dumpty," or "Old Mother Hubbard." Have children read aloud the rhyme. Talk about the story line of the rhyme. Model for children the directions to create a slit book (see page 41). Have children complete each step as you model it. Ask them to rewrite the rhyme as a story with a beginning, a middle, and an end. Invite children to illustrate their story in their slit book and use speech bubbles to add dialogue to the story.

Story to Play

Read aloud a fable such as *The Tortoise and the Hare.* Have children work in small groups to restructure the story as a play. Help them think of each character, what the character might say and do, and then create and write a short play based on the story. Invite children in each group to design simple story character headbands or costumes to wear and present their play to the class.

Picture Book to Super Story

For each child, fold a 9" x 12" (23 cm x 30.5 cm) piece of construction paper and two 8½" x 11" (21.5 cm x 28 cm) pieces of white paper in half widthwise. Place the folded blank sheets in the folded construction paper, and staple them together along the folded side to make a blank book. Give each child a blank book and a Goldilocks and the Three Bears reproducible (page 42). Have children tell the story of Goldilocks and the Three Bears, or read a version of the story to them. Then, ask children to cut out the pictures and glue one picture on each page of their blank book in sequential order. Have children use the pictures as a guide to retell and write the story. Invite children to color the pictures to complete their book.

Slit Book Directions

1. Fold a piece of paper in half lengthwise.

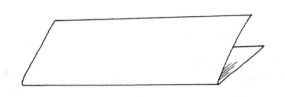

2. Open the paper and fold it in half widthwise. Then, fold it once more in the same direction.

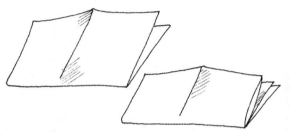

3. Open the paper to a half sheet. Starting from the folded edge, cut along the crease. Stop where the fold lines intersect.

4. Completely open the paper.

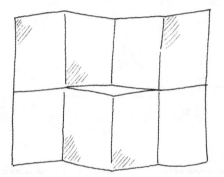

5. Fold the paper in half lengthwise.

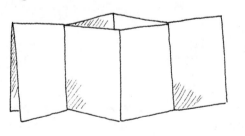

6. Grasp the outer edges as shown, and push them towards the center. The opening should "poof" out. Keep pushing until you have a book of four sections.

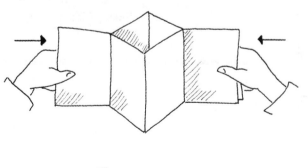

7. Fold the pages to make a book.

Balancing Literacy • K–2 © 2002 Creative Teaching Press

Goldilocks and the Three Bears

Balancing Literacy • K–2 © 2002 Creative Teaching Press

During modeled writing, the teacher and children collaborate to create text, but the teacher writes the text. To model writing, talk about the text and discuss the processes a writer should use. Model concepts about print, top to bottom, left-to-right writing, writing to a specific topic, and how and when to include punctuation. Write on chart paper, an overhead projector, or the chalkboard so that all children can see clearly. When children discuss and give input about the writing, they are participating in shared writing. Use these activities to incorporate modeled and shared writing into your daily schedule.

Daily Riddle

Use Daily Riddle as a whole-group activity to provide short, meaningful context through which children can develop reasoning skills and work on phonemic awareness and phonics skills (listen for patterns of sound to associate with patterns of print). This activity is based on children's current skill development. It should be simple in kindergarten and grow more complex by second grade. Use the directions for Riddle Me This! (page 46) to customize the activity for your class.

Morning Message—Chart Format

Use Morning Message as a whole-group activity to provide a written format to model the use of language for the purpose of sharing information. Morning Message is not an interactive writing activity, but you can use it in an interactive way to preview skills you will present during the week. Write the morning message on a permanent surface (e.g., chart paper) because children will use it later to practice phonics skills. Use the directions for You've Got Mail (page 48) to customize the activity for your class.

Morning Message—Speech Bubble Format

Another option for the Morning Message activity is to use the speech bubble format. Choose a mascot that correlates with your unit of study. The mascot can be a stuffed animal, a plastic figurine, or a drawing. Write the morning message on a paper speech bubble, and attach it to the mascot. Use the directions for Says Who? (page 50) to customize the activity for your class.

Daily News—Oral to Print Format

Use Daily News to model the use of children's own life experiences as a source of writing and reading. Daily News is a dynamic, whole-group, developmental writing strategy that changes over time as children mature in their understanding of the alphabetic principle. Children practice oral language, story summarization, finding the main idea, concepts about print, the alphabet, and letter formation during this activity. Use the directions for Dateline News (page 52) to customize the activity for your class.

Daily News—Category Format

Use this Daily News approach to have children practice oral language, categorization, concepts about print, phonemic awareness, alphabet awareness, synthetic phonics, and letter formation. Assist children in their move from only drawing pictures to represent their thoughts to the process of listening for sounds, identifying letters that represent those sounds, and then labeling their drawings. Use the directions for What's the Category? (page 54) to customize the activity for your class.

Daily News with an Editor

After you record children's news summaries, invite a volunteer to be the editor and check the daily news for any errors. Ask the editor to use correction tape to cover any mistakes and to make the corrections on the chart. Use the directions for Eagle Eyes News (page 56) to customize the activity for your class.

Skill Cards

Extend children's learning by providing "skill cards" for them to use with the writing samples the class created during shared writing activities. Write skills, letter blends, or sight words on separate index cards to make skill cards. Place the skill cards and a pack of small sticky notes in a basket. Place the basket in your Writing Area. When the class finishes a shared writing lesson, place the completed writing piece in the Writing Area. Invite children to choose a skill card from the basket and reread the morning message to practice the skill or pinpoint the blend or sight word noted on the card. For example, a child who picks a skill card that says *today* would place a piece of Wikki Stix around the word *today* on the Morning Message chart. Ask children to copy the word on a sticky note, "autograph" (write their name on the back of) the note, and place it on the chart.

If the shared writing activity is written on an overhead transparency, place the transparency in a plastic sleeve. Have children use an overhead marker to write on the transparency. For example, a child who picks a card that says *Find capital letters* would draw a circle around all the capital letters on the plastic sleeve.

Daily Riddle

Riddle Me This!

1 Copy the Daily Riddle reproducible (page 47) on an overhead transparency. Before children arrive, select a word family or vowel pattern (e.g., *ee*). Write a common word that contains the pattern on the blank line at the top of the reproducible to create a riddle (e.g., *What rhymes with <u>tree</u>?*). Draw a picture of the word in the box.

2 Read the riddle to the class.

3 Create a clapping rhythm, and read the riddle to the beat as an echo chant. Invite children to repeat it with you. Ask children to respond with a rhyming word. Children may say a word that has the pattern of sound but not the pattern of print (e.g., *flea*) or generate nonsense words (e.g., *pree*). Write children's responses on the transparency.

4 At the end of Daily Riddle, wipe off the children's responses, and place the transparency in a three-hole punched plastic sleeve. Place a metal ring through one of the holes, and hang the ring on a magnetic hook. Attach the hook to the overhead projector cart or your file cabinet. Place it in the Writing Area. During literacy center time, invite children to use overhead markers to write on the plastic sleeve a list of words that rhyme with the riddle word. Encourage children to read the words.

5 Then, have children use the My Word Sort reproducible (page 28) to sort their words into vowel pattern categories. (See Word Sorts on page 27.)

6 Ask children to use a damp paper towel to wipe the print off the plastic sleeve so it is clean for the next child to use.

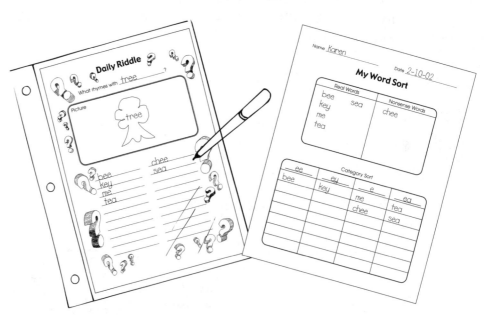

Daily Riddle

What rhymes with _____?

Picture

_____ _____
_____ _____
_____ _____
_____ _____
_____ _____
_____ _____

Balancing Literacy • K–2 © 2002 Creative Teaching Press

Modeled and Shared Writing

Morning Message

You've Got Mail

1 Copy the Morning Message reproducible (page 49) on an overhead transparency, or write the text shown on the reproducible on chart paper to create an enlarged version.

2 Before children arrive, write a message on the chart or transparency by filling in the blanks. Write the date and weather, a statement of one or two important events of the day, and sign your name. As an option, add rebus drawings to complement the text. Place the chart next to the class calendar. Use the chart and calendar together to reinforce print concepts (e.g., reading from left to right), to help children find the date on the calendar, and to have them discuss the weather.

3 Read the message to the class, and then reread it with them. Track each word as you read. (For second graders, track line by line instead of word by word.) After reading, select and highlight one or two skills (e.g., capitalization and phonics skills). Use Wikki Stix, colored markers, or highlighting tape to focus on these skills in the morning message.

4 At the end of the Morning Message, place the chart or transparency in the Writing Area with a small basket of skill cards (see page 45) and sticky notes. Invite children to use the cards to practice skills and locate letter blends and/or sight words in the morning message.

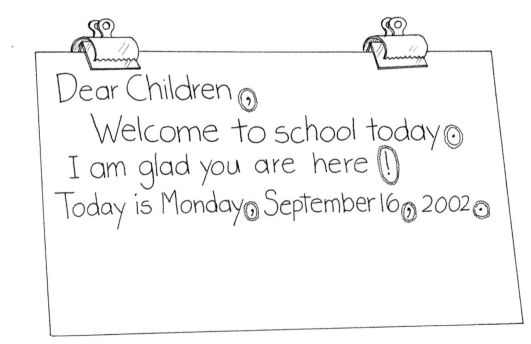

Morning Message

Dear Children,

Welcome to school today.

I am glad you are here!

Today is _____, _____, 200___.

The weather is _____.

Today we will _____

_____.

Have a great day!

Your teacher,

_____

Morning Message

Say's Who?

1. Copy the Speech Bubble reproducible (page 51), and laminate it.

2. Before children arrive, write a message on a piece of paper. Include one or two new content vocabulary words in the message. Create the message for children as if the unit mascot (see page 44) had written it to the class. For example, use a stuffed bear as a mascot for a unit of study on bears in winter. Attach the piece of paper to the speech bubble, or use an overhead pen or a dark crayon to write directly on the laminated bubble. (Use tissue and water to erase ink. Cut off the foot section of an old pair of pantyhose to create a "mitt," and use it to erase crayon markings.)

3. Place the mascot on a stool near the chalkboard, and place the tip of the speaking bubble in the mascot's mouth with a safety pin so that it looks like the bubble is attached to the mascot. Attach the back of the bubble to the board.

4. Read the message to the class, and then reread it with them. Track each word as you read. After reading, highlight the new vocabulary words and one or two other skills that relate to print concepts, phonics, or sight words. End the activity by using Wikki Stix, colored markers, or highlighting tape to focus on the skills.

5. Place the bubble message in the Writing Area. Invite children to review the message and use the skill cards (see page 45) to practice sight word recognition and phonics skills.

Speech Bubble

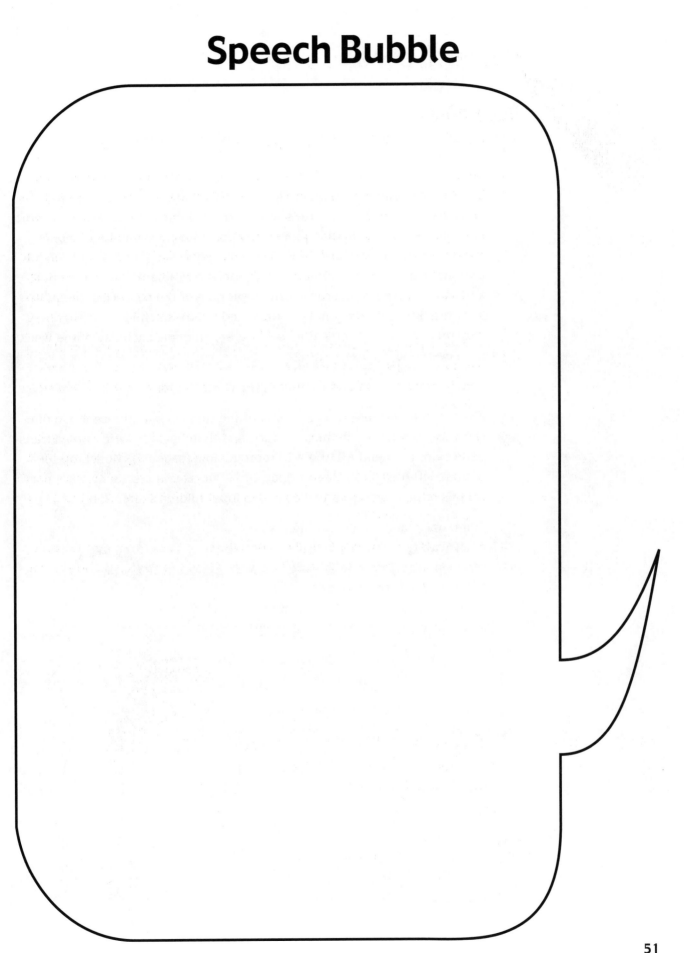

Modeled and Shared Writing

Daily News

Dateline News

1 Assign a color to each day of the school week, and assign each child to a color group. Tell children they will be "reporters" for one day during the week. For example, Robby is in the green group and the green group members are the daily reporters on Thursdays. Explain to parents that on their assigned day the daily reporters will share with the rest of the class a short story about something that happened to them or their family members. Have approximately four or five children report each day. If your schedule does not permit this much time, write each child's name on a craft stick, and place the sticks in a can. At the beginning of the day, select the number of sticks for which you have time, and tell those children so that they may prepare their reports. Choose different students each day of the week until everyone has had a turn.

2 Ask the reporter to stand in front of the class and tell his or her own story.

3 After each report, use the main idea of the story to paraphrase it in a one-sentence summary. Say the summary, and then begin to write it on a transparency of the Read All About It! reproducible (page 53). Model top-to-bottom, left-to-right print concepts, and write as you restate the summary. Do this rather quickly so you do not to lose children's attention.

4 Point, track, and read the written summary with the class. Then, call on the next reporter. Continue this process with the rest of that day's reports. (Note: Write all reports for that day on the same Read All About It! transparency.)

5 Invite one of the daily reporters to draw a picture on the transparency.

6 At the end of the activity, place the transparency and a basket of skill cards (see page 45) in the Writing Area. Invite children to review the transparency and use the skill cards to practice sight word recognition and phonics skills.

7 A fun option is to play "news beat" music and have a "special reporter jacket" for the reporters to wear and a pretend microphone for them to speak into.

Read All About It!

Our Class News
by Room ____

Date: _____

_____
_____
_____
_____
_____
_____
_____
_____
_____
_____
_____
_____

Balancing Literacy • K–2 © 2002 Creative Teaching Press

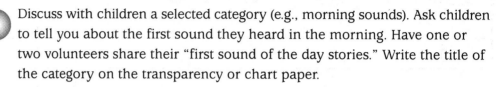

Daily News

What's the Category?

1 Copy the What's the Category? reproducible (page 55) on an overhead transparency, or write the text shown on the reproducible on chart paper.

2 Discuss with children a selected category (e.g., morning sounds). Ask children to tell you about the first sound they heard in the morning. Have one or two volunteers share their "first sound of the day stories." Write the title of the category on the transparency or chart paper.

3 Model your thinking process by slowly saying the first sound you heard in the morning. For example, if you heard your neighbor's dog barking, slowly say *dog.* Quickly sketch a dog under "My Picture."

4 Say the word again, and highlight the beginning sound. Ask *What sound do you hear in the beginning of the word **dog**?* (/d/) Direct children's attention to an alphabet chart, and slowly sing each sound for each letter, starting with *a.* Stop at the letter *d,* and identify /d/ as the sound that starts the word *dog.*

5 Write the letter *d* under "Sounds and Letters in My Word." Explain your writing process to create the letter. For example, say *I am writing the letter **d**. I make a curve and a straight line going down.*

6 Review what you have written. Touch the picture of the dog, say *dog,* touch the letter *d,* and say /d/. Then, slowly say each sound as you write *dog* under "My Word."

7 Remind the class what one of the children said about the first sound of the day, and repeat the process with his or her contribution.

8 Another option is to have children listen for ending or middle sounds. Write the word under "Sounds and Letters in My Word," but omit the letter that makes the target sound. For example, write __og for *dog* when your target sound is /d/. Then, use the process described above to have children listen for and identify the missing letter.

9 Remember, this is not a laborious process. Quickly complete the steps to keep children's attention focused on the chart and your modeling of this strategic process.

What's the Category?

_____

My Picture	Sounds and Letters in My Word	My Word

Daily News

Eagle Eyes News

1. Copy the News Beat reproducible (page 57) on an overhead transparency.

2. Ask a volunteer to be a "reporter" and prepare and deliver a short news report in one or two sentences. The "news" can be something that happened in the classroom (e.g., *Our class frog laid eggs*) or something personal that happened in a classmate's life (e.g., *Sally's mom had a baby*). Invite the reporter to state his or her news. Write the report on the transparency. Include mistakes based on current skills study. For example, if the class is learning about punctuation marks, omit some commas and periods in the written report. Display the transparency.

3. Have the reporter choose another child to be an "editor." Encourage the editor to find and correct all mistakes (e.g., capitalization, punctuation, spelling) or "trick" the rest of the class by leaving one or two for them to find. If the class knows this is an option, the editor will not suffer embarrassment if he or she happens to overlook a mistake.

4. Ask the class to vote on whether all errors were corrected. Have the editor place a star under the "Edit Complete" section of the transparency when all the mistakes have been corrected.

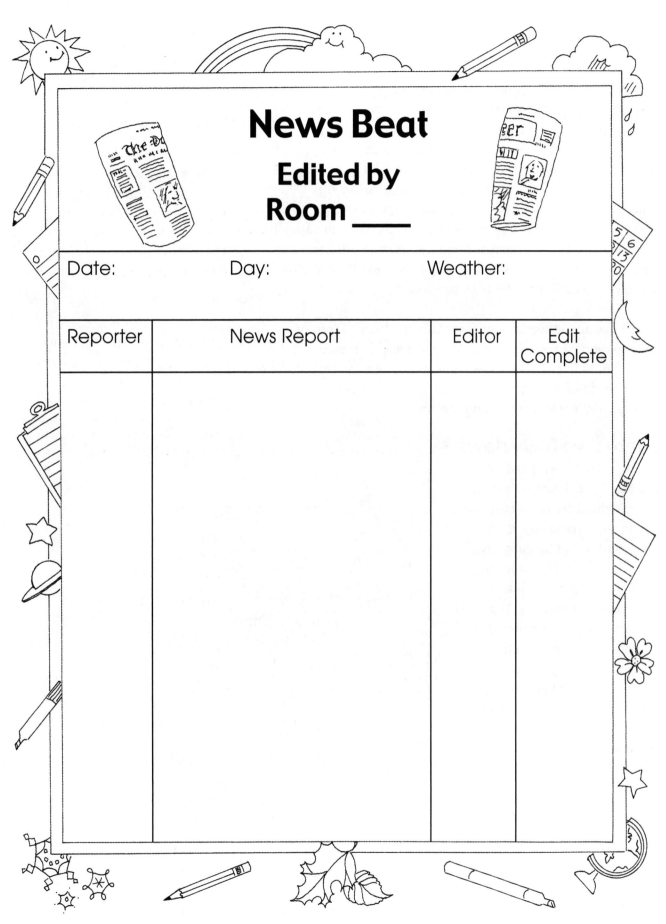

News Beat
Edited by
Room ____

Date:	Day:		Weather:

Reporter	News Report	Editor	Edit Complete

With interactive and guided writing, the teacher guides a small group or works one-on-one with children to teach them about the writing process and about how written language works. The teacher and children create meaningful text together as they "share the pen." The teacher can extend this supportive process to also help children express what they want to say in their writing. Mini-lessons on specific writing skills such as when to capitalize letters, how to correctly use punctuation marks, how to develop various types of sentence structure (e.g., simple, compound), and how to write paragraphs can also be presented through these processes.

Interactive and guided writing build upon what children have learned from class participation, shared reading, and language experiences. Display text created during an interactive writing session so children can repeatedly read the text. The goal is to create together writing that follows conventional standards of grammar, punctuation, capitalization, and spelling.

Interactive Daily News

During this activity, children and teacher will share the pen to write the daily news based on children's experiences. Children will practice oral language, concepts about print, phonics skills, sight word recognition, and conventions of writing. This type of interactive writing provides a bridge to support children between whole-group shared writing and small-group interactive writing. Use the What's Up? activity on page 59 to incorporate interactive and guided writing in your daily schedule.

Interactive Daily News

What's Up?

1 Choose five children to be class "reporters" for the week. Each day, ask one reporter to think of some type of "news" he or she would like to share with the class. The news can be something that has happened to the child at home or something that relates to someone else at school. Then, summarize and identify the main idea of the report. For example, Jana could say *Yesterday, I came home from school and I saw my cat lying on the floor. My cat was sick. My mom said we have to take her to the veterinarian.* Summarize Jana's report by saying *Did you hear that boys and girls? Jana's cat is sick.*

2 Write the date and the summary sentence (e.g., *Jana's cat is sick*) on a piece of chart paper. Pause for children to spell some of the words or to share the pen and write them on the paper. For some words, identify letter sounds, and ask volunteers to write the letter(s) that represent those sounds.

3 After writing each sentence, stop to have the class read it together. Check to determine if all words and punctuation marks are correct. Use correction tape (white masking tape) or sticky notes to cover the mistakes. Then, make the necessary corrections with children's help. Think aloud as to why each correction needs to be made and how it should be done.

4 Each day, place the completed chart in the Writing Area for children to revisit. Invite them to use the charts with the skill cards (see page 45). At the end of the week, bind all of the charts together inside a cover. Allow volunteers to decorate the cover. Add the book to the Reading Area for children to read. It makes a wonderful "diary" of classroom experiences.

Independent Writing

Children can generate independent writing from books they read together in class, independent research on topics of interest, or life experiences. Usually, independent writing requires little teacher support. Children create their own messages, stories, labels, and lists using known words and invented words based on their current level of understanding of the alphabetic principle. They may refer to word walls, charts, dictionaries, word banks, or the computer as sources of help with conventional spelling.

Use journal writing, reader response activities, letter writing, and creative story writing to give children independent writing opportunities. Have them complete independent writing assignments in the Writing Area during center time.

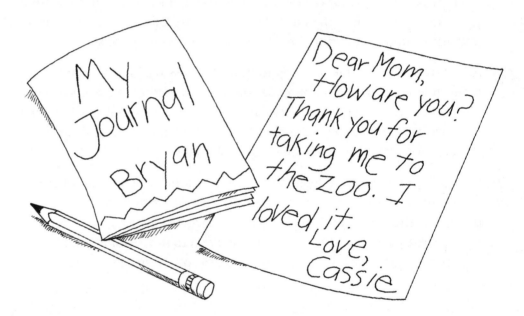

Portfolios

Give each child a writing portfolio. Have children keep writing samples from throughout the school year in their folder. Invite children to choose the work samples, complete a For My Portfolio reproducible (page 119) for each sample, attach it to the sample, and place the samples in their portfolio.

By carefully examining children's independent writing, you can better assess where each child is in the developmental writing continuum and more effectively plan for writing mini-lessons to present during whole-group or small-group sessions or during guided reading with a child on a one-on-one basis.

Journal Writing

Journals offer children an opportunity for risk-free personal writing. Introduce journal writing on the first day of school, and include it in the class schedule each day. Children learn to write and write well by writing! Early on, have children write about their own experiences at home, at school, or in the community. Later, ask them to write about stories they have read and make connections from story characters to their own life. Help children generate writing topics, but do not assign topics. Do not grade the journals. Instead, use them to assess where your children are as writers, what their strengths are, and where their weaknesses lie.

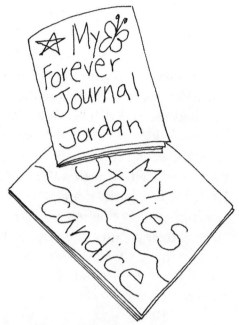

Staple several pieces of paper together to make journals, or have children use spiral bound notebooks or composition books. Personal ownership is the key to successful journals, so it is important to let young writers choose their favorite writing instrument and decorate their journal covers.

Customize journal writing according to grade level. Younger learners in kindergarten and first grade have short attention spans, so periods of 5–15 minutes at a time are adequate. Their eye-hand coordination is developing, but their fine motor control is limited, so having them write at journal time and then again during literacy center time is preferable to having them write for one long period. Have children begin by drawing pictures as a form of written expression and then move along the developmental writing "trail" as their knowledge base expands and their skills improve. Children in second grade can handle 15–30 minutes for journal writing. They are beginning to move from invented spelling to conventional spelling and their stories are more elaborate. Give them journals to which they can add pages so they can extend their stories.

Several types of journals are appropriate for young writers, but do not plan to use all of them at once. Vary the types of journals used with your classroom projects and topics of study. Use the activities on pages 62–63 to engage children in journal writing.

Journal Writing

My Draw and Tell Journal

Staple several blank sheets of paper together to create a journal for each child. This type of journal provides children with an opportunity to view themselves as writers because they can draw pictures as a form of written communication. As children learn about letter and sound connections, have them label their pictures with letter strings, words, phrases, and then sentences. When children are correctly labeling their pictures, they are ready to move to the My Stories journal format (see below). (kindergarten, early first grade)

My Stories

For each child, copy the My Stories reproducible (page 64) and attach it to several pieces of blank paper to create a journal. Invite children to write about their own life stories in their journal. This type of journal is like a diary, so share entries at children's discretion. Encourage children to write first and then illustrate their writing (Note: In the beginning, children may do the reverse.) As children feel more secure with their writing, they will begin to write and then illustrate. Provide diecuts and stencils of objects related to the topic of study to give kindergarten and first-grade children a pattern to copy. Have children glue the diecut in place or trace the stencil, quickly draw background scenery, and then write. (late kindergarten, first and second grades)

Journal Writing

My Learning Log

For each child, copy the My Learning Log reproducible (page 65) and attach it to several pieces of blank paper to create a journal. Ask children to informally write about what they have learned during the reading of a nonfiction book, during a unit of study, or after independent research in science or social studies. Invite them to observe various classroom objects (e.g., the class pets, growing plants) and report their findings in a class learning log. Or, give each child an individual log to write in for the duration of the unit of study. (late kindergarten, first and second grades)

Literature Response Journal

Ask children to respond to stories they read individually or during small- or whole-group time or to stories that have been read to the class. Prompt responses by asking children questions about character, setting, story plot, or other story elements. (late kindergarten, first and second grades)

My Forever Journal

A school-to-home journal allows parents to respond to children's work. Toward the end of each day, have children write one or two sentences that reflect the most important thing they learned that day—the thing they hope to remember forever. Each day, have children place their journal in their backpack and take it home. Tell them to ask their parents to read their journal and then initial or sign the entry or write comments about it. Have children return their journal to school each day. (kindergarten, first and second grades)

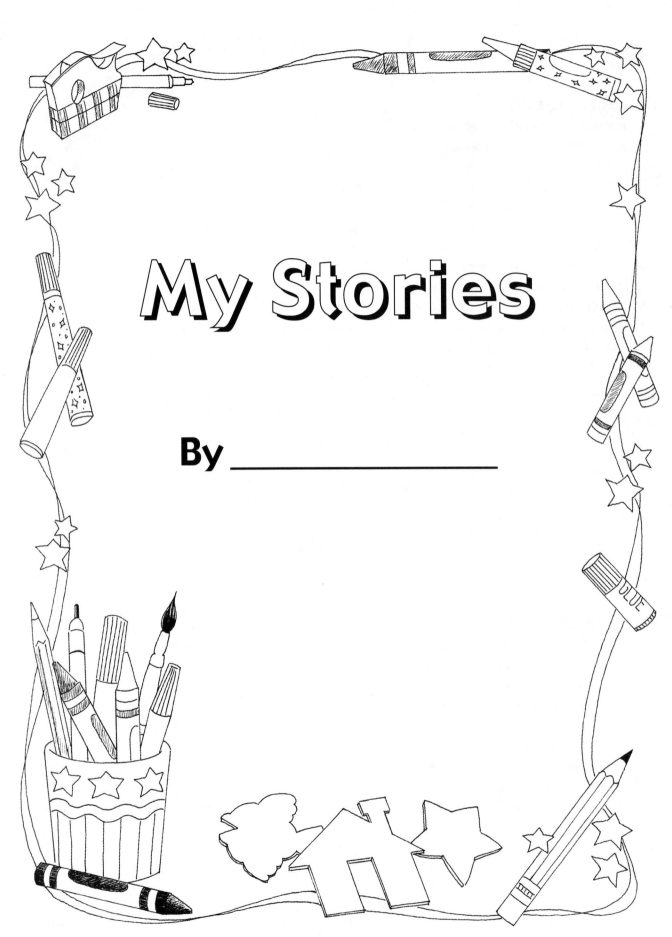

My Stories

By _____

Balancing Literacy • K–2 © 2002 Creative Teaching Press

My Learning Log

By _____

The Writing Process

The writing process is a systematic way to introduce writing skills and develop children's writing abilities. The five steps include prewriting, drafting, revising, editing, and publishing. Separately introduce each step to young writers, and make sure they have learned each step before adding the next step. Prewriting and drafting make up the majority of the writing experiences for children in kindergarten and the first half of first grade. However, model the other steps in a whole-group setting so children can experience the whole process. Tell a story, write the story, and follow all five steps of the writing process with the group to create a class Big Book.

Have children in the second half of first grade and in second grade participate in all five steps of the process. First, model the process to the whole class, and then have them develop their journal stories into published pieces. Children who have had a great deal of experience with the Daily News formats (see page 44) are better prepared to write; they have an understanding of where a story idea comes from, what it needs to include, and how to develop it.

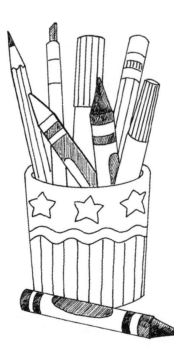

Children practice these skills during the writing process:

1. Prewriting—writers organize their thoughts about their writing subject before they actually write

2. Drafting—writers use prewriting details to write complete sentences

3. Revising—writers reread their story and think about changes that would improve their story

4. Editing—writers check for spelling, capitalization, and punctuation errors

5. Publishing—writers neatly rewrite or type their stories and add illustrations to accompany their text

Use the activity described on the following pages to introduce children to the writing process.

Step 1: Prewriting Activity

1. Read aloud a nonfiction book about an animal.

2. Ask children to talk about their favorite animals.

3. Give each child a Brainstorm Web reproducible (page 69), and ask children to draw a picture of their favorite animal in the oval.

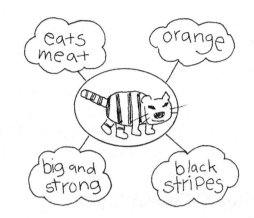

4. Refer back to the animal book, and talk about the animal's characteristics, its color and size, what it can do, what it eats, and where it lives. Ask children to think about their favorite animal and its color and size, activities, food, and habitat.

5. Have children draw on their web pictures that represent each of the four categories discussed in step 4. Ask them to label their drawings with words and phrases. Explain to children that this process is one way to organize their thoughts about their writing topic before they start writing.

Step 2: Drafting Activity

1. Have children use their prewriting details to write a story about their animal. Ask children to skip a line between each sentence so there will be space for any revisions or comments.

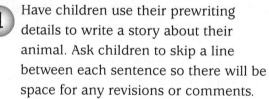

2. Invite children to use their invented spelling and knowledge of sight words during this step. Children will make decisions about spelling and punctuation during the next steps. The goal at this step is for children to write about the ideas they developed during the prewriting step.

Step 3: Revising Activity

1. Have children reread their story and think about changes that would make it better. Invite them to add, delete, or reorganize their sentences to make a complete story with a beginning, a middle, and an end.

2. Encourage them to add interesting details, use more vivid language and descriptors, and delete sentences that may not add to the story or that are off topic.

Step 4: Editing Activity

 Have children check for spelling, capitalization, and punctuation errors and circle any words that do not "look right" or that they want to look up.

 Invite them to look at one or more classroom resources (e.g., word wall, word bank, dictionary) to check their spelling. Have children exchange stories with a peer for another edit and then show their story to you for a writer–teacher conference and the final edit.

Step 5: Publishing Activity

 Give each child a My Favorite Animal reproducible (page 70), and ask children to neatly rewrite their story. Or, invite children to type their story on the computer.

 Invite children to draw a picture to illustrate their story and attach their story to their illustration for final publication.

Culminating Activity Ideas

 Invite children to share their story with teachers, parents, friends, and class-mates. Place all finished stories in the Reading Area for all to enjoy.

2 Tape-record each student author reading his or her story on one cassette. Combine all the student stories to make a class book. Place the cassette and the book in a resealable plastic bag. Place the bag at the Listening Post Area, and invite children to listen to the tape as they read the book.

3 Invite children to attend an "authors' tea." Make a copy of the Authors' Tea Program reproducible (page 71). Write the names of six student authors who would like to share their story. Make enough copies of the completed reproducible to give one to each audience member. The audience will include the rest of the class and any parents, other classes, or administrators you choose to invite. For extra fun, serve tea (or another beverage) in plastic teacups.

Brainstorm Web

My Favorite Animal

_____

_____

_____

_____

_____

_____

_____

_____

_____

_____

By _____

Balancing Literacy • K–2 © 2002 Creative Teaching Press

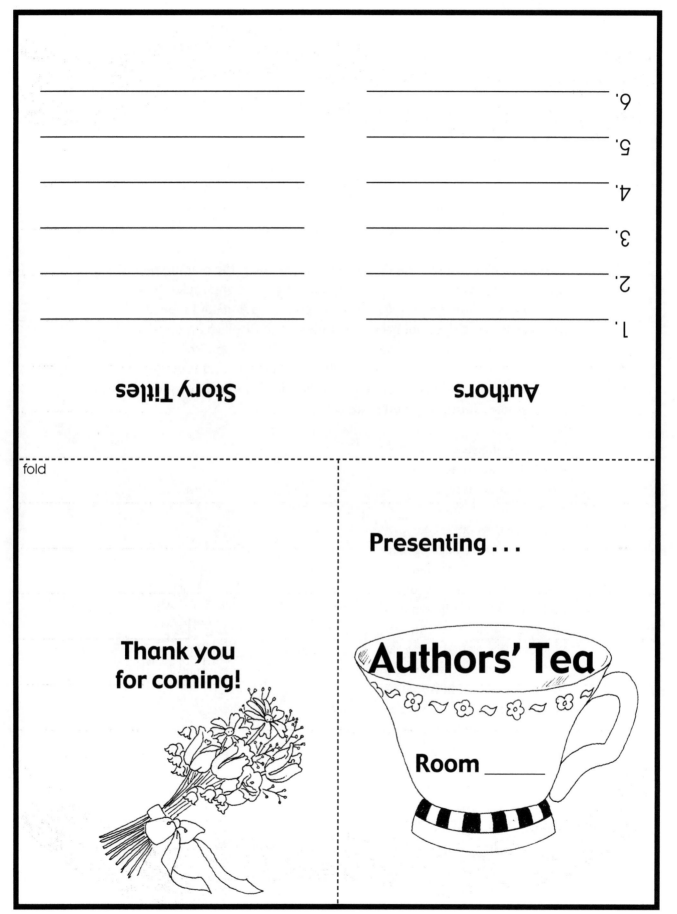

(Story Titles)

1.

2.

3.

4.

5.

6.

Story Titles

(Authors)

1.

2.

3.

4.

5.

6.

Authors

fold

Thank you
for coming!

Presenting . . .

Authors' Tea

Room _____

Balancing Literacy • K–2 © 2002 Creative Teaching Press

Reading

Reading is a developmental process that children become more proficient at over time and with practice. Children need to read and be read to every day. Children need to use the background knowledge they bring to the reading experience along with their vocabulary knowledge and their understanding of word order or grammar. To read independently, they must conquer the alphabetic code.

To provide children with all they need to launch into the reading process, model reading with expression, read from all genres, and make materials available for whole-group reading, small-group reading, and individual practice. Reading does not occur just in books so display charts, post directions and instructions, and label objects in the classroom. Provide a comfortable area for quiet reading time. Display books of various genres in the Reading Area, but include nonfiction books and materials in your science, social studies, music, art, and math centers as well.

The following section presents information about the developmental stages of reading, and describes the characteristics and needs of children at each stage of reading. Use the Developmental Stages of Reading chart on page 73 to determine which stage each child is at and provide children with appropriate activities to meet their needs. In addition to the information on reading stages, this section also contains reading strategies and numerous reading formats that provide a great variety of models to enrich children's reading experiences. These formats include modeled and shared reading, guided reading, independent reading, and Story Circles.

Developmental Stages of Reading

The following lists describe the characteristics and needs of children at each developmental stage of reading.

Stage	Characteristics	Needs
Emergent Readers (Early and Upper-Emergent Level)	• Enjoy being read to and will often ask to hear the same story over and over • Imitate reading-like behaviors learned from observing reading styles of teachers, parents, or siblings • Begin to discover the connection between oral and written language • Use their own language to tell a story but "borrow" text from books previously read • Begin to discover that they can read the same words in many different formats and books	• Print-rich environment where independent reading is scaffolded and encouraged • Many opportunities to hear rich literature being read by teachers, visitors, older children, and reading buddies and in tape-recorded stories during listening center time • Many opportunities to respond to literature in multimodal ways using rhythm, rhyme, art, music, and drama • Participation in shared, modeled, and interactive reading and writing • Skill instruction should be systematic and explicit but should always focus on meaning and be connected to meaningful reading opportunities—songs, poems, chants, books, and environmental print, including the word wall
Developing Readers (Early-Fluency Level)	• Begin to gain control over many decoding and word recognition skills • Becoming risk-takers with unfamiliar material • Use multiple cues, including semantic, graphophonic, and syntactic cues to read for fluency and comprehension • Use knowledge of oral language to correct miscues when reading • Begin to talk about their strategy use during reading • Write in response to literature • Read self-selected books for enjoyment	• Many opportunities to enjoy and respond to literature • Numerous shared and choral reading experiences • To focus on comprehension strategies • To develop higher-level thinking skills • To simultaneously develop reading and writing skills. • Many opportunities to retell stories, create story maps, write innovations (rewrites) of text, and explore expository (nonfiction) materials
Independent Readers (Fluency Level)	• Read with minimal guidance or without assistance • Read more complex material • Begin to read with a critical eye • Use background knowledge and experience to predict actions and elements of the story • Develop new ways to solve reading and writing problems	• Time to read with others and to talk about their ideas to expand upon the meaning of the text • Many opportunities to preview books, set purposes for reading, predict and confirm ideas, explore possibilities, make inferences, and draw conclusions • Opportunities to participate in book discussions to examine story elements and events • Time to develop story innovations and to respond to reading in journals

Reading Strategies

Reading strategies are ways for children to "lift" the print off the paper, examine the illustrations, think about what they know about the reading situation, and synthesize all of that information to make meaning. Most children need explicit modeling of the reading strategies. Use meaningful text in an actual reading situation to model the strategies. Once children are familiar with them they will be able to take action to solve their problem when they come to a roadblock in their reading.

To read for meaning, children need to access information from several cues (as shown below).

A **Semantics** (also known as the "meaning cue")
Components
- Background knowledge
- Knowledge of "story"
- Knowledge of language/vocabulary

B **Syntactics** (also known as the "structure cue")
Components
- Syntax, word order, or grammar
- Syntax for various types of text

C **Graphophonics** (also known as the "visual cue")
Components
- Sound awareness (phonemic awareness)
- Visual/letter/word awareness
- Sound/symbol correspondence

D **Schema**
Components
- Backdrop for all transactions with text
- Activated before, during, and after reading

Strategic Reading Development

Teach children the following strategies during guided reading and shared reading sessions, and encourage children to use them daily.

1 Activate prior knowledge.
- Check for picture clues.
- Think about what you already know about the subject or author.

2 Look carefully at unknown words.
- Analyze the word. (Use "within-word" clues such as knowledge of sound–symbol matchings and word family patterns, vowel patterns, and sight words.)
- Chunk large words into recognizable parts.

3 Deal with the "tricky" part of the story.
- Read past it. (Use think pads and pencils.)
- Use context clues to figure it out.
- Reread the word in context (use "within context" clues) and focus on meaning.

4 Think aloud about what is known to help figure out the unknown. (reading by analogy)

5 Self-monitor to self-correct during reading.

Modeled Reading

Modeled reading is the process of reading aloud to children at a higher listening level. During modeled reading, children hear a story being read with expression and fluency—a story that contains more sophisticated vocabulary and syntax patterns than children's instructional text. During the read-aloud, children and teacher engage in meaningful conversation about the ideas in the story and about the characters, setting, main events, and other items of interest to further children's story comprehension.

Teacher read-alouds are great opportunities for modeled reading, so carefully choose books from a variety of genres and authors to read to your class. Spend at least 15 minutes per day reading to children. At the end of the reading period, have children talk about and summarize the portion of the story read that day and make predictions about what will happen next. Read-alouds foster children's enthusiasm for books and a sincere love of reading.

Choosing a Book

There are so many wonderful children's books to choose from. How do you decide which ones to read to your class? Select books that are related to your current unit of study, including books that may be too sophisticated for children to read independently. Read aloud nonfiction books to present information that children would be unable to obtain from their independent reading. Be sure to read books from a variety of genres, including multicultural literature, poetry, autobiographies, biographies, legends, myths, folktales, fables, fantasy, historical fiction, mysteries, and realistic fiction. Choose picture books and simple chapter books to read aloud. The following pages feature suggested read-aloud books in a variety of genres.

Suggested Read-Aloud Books

Multicultural Books

Abuela by Arthur Dorros (Dutton)

Children Just Like Me: Celebrations! by Anabel Kindersley (DK Publishing)

Everybody Cooks Rice by Norah Dooley (Lerner Publishing Group)

Jin Woo by Eve Bunting (Clarion Books)

Oranges on Golden Mountain by Elizabeth Partridge (Dutton)

Sadako and the Thousand Paper Cranes by Eleanor Coerr (Putnam)

Why Mosquitoes Buzz in People's Ears by Verna Aardema (Econo-Clad Books)

Poetry

A Light in the Attic by Shel Silverstein (HarperCollins)

Pass It On: African-American Poetry for Children selected by Wade Hudson (Scholastic)

The Random House Book of Poetry for Children by Jack Prelutsky (Random House)

Read-Aloud Rhymes for the Very Young by Jack Prelutsky (Alfred A. Knopf Books)

Sing a Song of Popcorn selected by Beatrice Schenk de Regniers (Scholastic)

Where the Sidewalk Ends by Shel Silverstein (HarperCollins)

Biographies

Ludwig Van Beethoven by Mike Venezia (Children's Press)

Picasso by Mike Venezia (Children's Press)

A Picture Book of Abraham Lincoln by David Adler (Holiday House)

A Picture Book of George Washington by David Adler (Holiday House)

Wilma Unlimited by Kathleen Krull (Voyager)

Suggested Read-Aloud Books

Caldecott Award Winners

Fables by Arnold Lobel (HarperCollins)

Grandfather's Journey by Allen Say (Houghton Mifflin)

Joseph Had a Little Overcoat by Simms Taback (Viking)

Jumanji by Chris Van Allsburg (Houghton Mifflin)

Officer Buckle and Gloria by Peggy Rathmann (Putnam)

The Snowy Day by Ezra Jack Keats (Viking)

Sylvester and the Magic Pebble by William Steig (Windmill Books)

Where the Wild Things Are by Maurice Sendak (HarperCollins)

Historical Fiction

Aunt Harriet's Underground Railroad in the Sky by Faith Ringgold (Econo-Clad Books)

The Courage of Sarah Noble by Alice Dalgliesh (Simon & Schuster)

Goin' Someplace Special by Patricia C. McKissack (Atheneum Books)

In 1492 by Jean Marzollo (Scholastic)

Katie and Mona Lisa by James Mayhew (Orchard Books)

Little Prairie House by Laura Ingalls Wilder (HarperCollins)

Other Favorites

Alexander and the Terrible, Horrible, No Good, Very Bad Day by Judith Viorst (Atheneum Books)

Blueberries for Sal by Robert McCloskey (Viking)

Frog and Toad Are Friends by Arnold Lobel (HarperCollins)

The Grouchy Ladybug by Eric Carle (HarperCollins)

Is Your Mama a Llama? by Deborah Guarino (Scholastic)

The Kissing Hand by Audrey Penn (Child Welfare League of America)

Martha Speaks by Susan Meddaugh (Houghton Mifflin)

Miss Spider's Tea Party by David Kirk (Scholastic)

The Napping House by Audrey Wood (Harcourt)

The Rainbow Fish by Marcus Pfister (North-South Books)

Tikki Tikki Tembo by Arlene Mosel (Henry Holt and Company)

When Sophie Gets Angry—Really, Really Angry . . . by Molly Bang (Scholastic)

Shared reading is an important process in the early-childhood classroom. It builds a community of readers in which all children are successful. Shared reading sessions provide a supportive reading experience in which teacher and children read enlarged text together to promote reading strategies, increase awareness of print concepts, build sight word vocabulary, and develop reading fluency. As the teacher reads a poem, song, or repetitive story to the whole class, children listen and then participate more fully with each rereading until they can read it independently.

Since everyone must have access to the text during the reading, use enlarged text such as Big Books, charts, sentence strips and word cards in pocket charts, and transparencies on the overhead projector. Use a variety of materials such as poems, songs, chants, nonfiction books, and stories. Choose books children will be interested in. The complete shared reading procedure is described in the following pages.

Reading Warm-Up

Choose two new ideas per week in kindergarten and first grade and one new selection per week in second grade. The warm-up provides short reading formats with which all children will be successful.

 Choose a song, chant, rap, poem, or nursery rhyme. (See pages 82–85 for suggested selections.)

 Introduce the selection to the class.

Write the selection on an overhead transparency or a piece of chart paper. Read the selection with children.

Revisit the selection each day of the week. Present it in a different format each day so children will recognize sight words and content words in different places. Gradually, children will be able to independently read the song or poem. The following is a suggested weekly schedule:

Monday—oral presentation with movement (if appropriate)
Tuesday—overhead transparency
Wednesday—large chart
Thursday—pocket chart with sentence strips and word cards
Friday—individual copy for each child's song and poem folder

 Once children are familiar with the song or poem, use it to teach specific skills. Choose a skill, according to a scope and sequence. Explicitly teach the skill to children, and then focus on the skill as you reread the poem.

 For each child, fold a 12" x 18" (30.5 cm x 46 cm) piece of construction paper in half lengthwise and copy the My Song and Poem Folder reproducible (page 86). Glue the reproducible to the front of the folded paper to make a folder for each child. Ask children to place their copies of the songs and poems in their folder.

Familiar Big Books

 Choose a Big Book to use to teach reading skills.

2 Invite children to talk about the cover to have them tap into prior knowledge, build schema, and make predictions.

3 Discuss the title and author with the class.

4 Read aloud the story to model enthusiasm and expression. Point to words or to lines of text as you read. Pause at prediction points, and ask children to predict what will happen next.

5 After reading the story, talk about it to build personal connections, and ask open-ended questions.

6 Suggestions for other lessons include the following:
- Identify parts of the book (cover, title, author, illustrator)
- Develop left-to-right directionality
- Match key words or text "chunks" to the story text
- Develop concepts of grammar, capitalization, and punctuation
- Build sound/symbol associations
- Develop a list of words with a target pattern, compound words, or root words with suffixes
- Develop a list of key vocabulary words

Repeated Reading Formats

Reread Big Book selections with children. Use any of the following methods when rereading:

- Echo chant (teacher says a line, children echo the same line)

- Call and response

- Whisper the text

- Clap words or phrases (syllable clapping)

- Use sound effects

- Use body movement or body percussion

- Read in parts/characters

- Pantomime or use dramatic role-play to retell the story

- Sing the text

Follow-up Activities

After children are familiar with a shared reading selection, have them respond to the reading. The more meaningful a follow-up activity is, the more interest the child will have. Here are some suggested follow-up activities:

- Present an oral retelling

- Create a puppet show

- Role-play the story

- Tape-record their reading of the story with sound effects

- Create class Big Books based on the story

- Create individual books

- Create a story on large paper to display on the wall

- Create a story on an overhead transparency

- Create story maps (see page 87)

- Write a letter to the author or a character

- Create character mobiles (see page 88)

- Create word charts (rhyming, vowel patterns, synonyms, etc.)

- Create an art response to the story

- Create a new ending for the story and compare the two endings

Use the Daily Shared Reading Plan reproducible (page 89) as a guideline when planning your shared reading lessons.

Down by the Bay

Down by the bay,

Where the watermelons grow,

Back to my home I dare not go.

For if I do, my mother will say,

"Did you ever see a whale with a polka-dot tail?"

Down by the bay.

2. Did you ever see a bear combing his hair?

3. Did you ever see a goose kissing a moose?

4. Did you ever see a fly wearing a tie?

5. Did you ever see a frog dancing with a dog?

Balancing Literacy • K–2 © 2002 Creative Teaching Press

Sing a Song of Sixpence

Sing a song of sixpence,
A pocket full of rye,
Four and twenty blackbirds
Baked in a pie.

When the pie was opened,
The birds began to sing.
Wasn't that a dainty dish
To set before the king?

The king was in his counting house
Counting out his money.
The queen was in the parlor
Eating bread and honey.

The maid was in the garden,
Hanging out the clothes,
When along came a blackbird
And snipped off her nose!

Balancing Literacy • K–2 © 2002 Creative Teaching Press

Miss Mary Mack
(from the traditional song)

Miss Mary Mack, Mack, Mack,
All dressed in black, black, black,
With silver buttons, buttons, buttons
All down her back, back, back.
She asked her mother, mother, mother
For fifteen cents, cents, cents
To see the elephant, elephant, elephant
Jump over the fence, fence, fence.
He jumped so high, high, high,
He touched the sky, sky, sky
And never came back, back, back
Till the Fourth of July-ly-ly.

Way Down South

Way down South where bananas grow,
A grasshopper stepped on an elephant's toe.
The elephant said with tears in his eyes,
"Pick on somebody your own size."

My Song and Poem Folder

By _____

Once Upon a Time . . .

Story Title _____

Characters

Setting _____

Problem _____

Main Events

1. _____

2. _____

3. _____

Solution _____

Name _____

Balancing Literacy • K–2 © 2002 Creative Teaching Press

Character Mobiles

Materials

crayons or markers
drawing paper
index cards
scissors

tape
wire coat hanger
string

1. Illustrate the main character in the story on drawing paper.

2. Brainstorm words that describe the character.

3. Write the words on index cards.

4. Cut out your drawing and tape it on a coat hanger.

5. Attach two pieces of string to the hanger. Tape the word cards to the strings.

Balancing Literacy • K–2 © 2002 Creative Teaching Press

Daily Shared Reading Plan

Warm-up Activities

(song) _____

(poem) _____

Familiar Selections

(Child's choice) _____

(Teacher's choice) _____

Mini Lesson(s)

Skills Lesson _____

Language Lesson _____

Story of the Week _____

Repeated Reading Format _____

Follow-up Activity _____

Independent Reading _____

Read-aloud Book _____

Balancing Literacy • K–2 © 2002 Creative Teaching Press

Guided Reading

Guided reading is a small-group instructional model that allows the teacher to select appropriate text for a small group of children (who are similar in strengths and needs) to provide instruction that targets specific reading strategies. The purpose of guided reading is to encourage independent reading. The focus is on mastery of reading strategies and elements of literature.

Organize children into groups of four to six based on their current reading skills. Give each child a copy of the same text. Have groups work with you or with each other to read text at their instructional level. Children's instructional level is when their accuracy rate for the reading is between 90–94%. 95–100% accuracy rate is mastery level, and below 89% accuracy is frustration level.

Complete the following tasks during guided reading:

● assess the developmental level of the children

● choose appropriate text and format for each reading level, and choose current strategy use of each group

● identify the focus reading strategies and appropriate skill work for each group

● constantly monitor and evaluate the children's progress using both formal (reading records) and informal (observational checklists) methods

The following pages describe a guided reading format and the processes involved.

The Guided Reading Lesson Format

The following pages describe a sample format to use for each guided reading lesson. Choose an appropriate book for your reading group, and follow the five steps.

 Story Introduction
- Read the title and the author and illustrator's names.
- Talk about the cover illustrations.

 Story Walk/Picture Talk
- Assess children's prior knowledge.
- Cover text if desired, and have children predict the story line through the pictures.
- Highlight and clarify concepts.
- Explain unusual language or language patterns.
- Model and call attention to appropriate reading strategies.

3 **First Reading**
- Teacher models reading. (Teacher has the only copy of the book.)
- Model the language patterns and concepts about print.
- Model the awareness and use of reading strategies.
- Children read silently. (Each child has a copy of the book.)
- Ask focus question.
- Guide children to silently read a selection.
- Discuss the meaning of text, and invite children to read aloud to confirm answers.

Second Reading (Each child has a copy of the book.)

- Choose one of the following options
  - ✔ Have children read aloud simultaneously.
  - ✔ Have children read quietly but simultaneously.
  - ✔ Ask children to read the story silently.
- Prompt and praise children's reading strategy use and awareness of concepts of print.
- Discuss the story.
  - ✔ Talk about the literary elements.
  - ✔ Talk about ideas and feelings about the story to connect it to children's lives.
  - ✔ Retell the story.
- Present the skill lesson.
  - ✔ Talk about concepts of print, vocabulary, and language structure.
  - ✔ Highlight sight words.
  - ✔ Discuss literary elements.

Independent Practice or Follow-up Activities

- Have children read independently or in pairs.
- Have children read chorally.
- Ask children to respond in writing.
- Have children participate in one or more follow-up activities. (See Follow-up Activities on page 81 for a list of ideas.)

During independent reading, children self-select text and read materials appropriate to their reading abilities. Independent reading, or practice reading, helps children become automatic with word recognition, extends their ability to read fluently with expression, and develops their love of books and reading as they read to become independent problem solvers.

Independent Reading

Sustained Silent Reading (S.S.R., or "Sorta Silent Reading" in kindergarten!) is one way to incorporate independent reading into your daily schedule. During this time, kindergarten children quietly browse books and first- and second-grade children silently read materials of their choice. There should be no interruptions, if possible, for children need to concentrate on their reading.

School-to-home connections are important so children continue reading independently for pleasure to develop the lifelong habit of reading for enjoyment and information. The following pages describe several take-home formats that are designed to build a solid relationship between the teacher and parents as partners with the child.

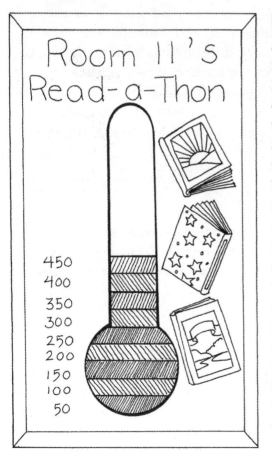

Books I Have Read

As a follow-up activity to independent reading time, give each child a Books I Have Read reproducible (page 95). Have children record the title of each book they read, write *fiction* or *nonfiction,* and record the date they completed the book. The more children read, the better they read, so encourage more independent reading by creating a class read-a-thon. Select a goal for the number of books to be read. For each child, staple together several copies of the Books I Have Read reproducible to make a reading log. Have children take home their logs each week to record any reading they do at home. Tally children's weekly reading totals, and record the class total on a bulletin board display. Do this weekly until the class reaches its read-a-thon goal.

Parents as Reading Partners

Explain to parents in letters or during con-
ferences and yearly meetings how important
it is for them to read to and with their children. Encourage them to listen to their children read independently. Explain that the
goal is for parents and children to read and
think about books together. Each week, have
children take home a Parent–Child Reading Conference Form (page 96) and a
book they selected for pleasure reading. Have children read and discuss the book
with their parents and then complete and sign the conference form. Encourage
parents to add their comments about the book to the form, draw their favorite
part, and then sign the form. Have children return the completed form to you.

Book Boxes

Encourage independent reading by making small books and library books available to children. Store the books in crates or boxes, and arrange the books by
theme and/or readability level.

Divide the class into reading groups, and place a set of leveled books in a separate box for each group. Assign each group a color, and color-code the boxes. Or,
give each group a name (e.g., Turtles), and write the group's name on their box.
Children will quickly learn which box contains books at their reading level,
which color represents recreational (i.e., fun, easy) reading, and which box contains books that present a challenge. Invite children to select books arranged by
theme even when the text is too complicated for them. Simply looking at the
pictures will help children study and think about the content in relation to what
they are learning in class. Allow children to choose from boxes that contain
books that are above and below their reading level. Reading easier material helps
children build their reading fluency, and they will benefit from the challenge of
reading more difficult books from time to time.

When children bring home books, parents do not
know which level the book is and may misunder-
stand if the child cannot read every word in the
book. Make several copies of the Bookmarks reproducible (page 97), and cut them apart. Give children
the appropriate bookmark to place in the book they
selected to take home. The bookmark will let parents
know whether they should have their child read the
book, read it with their child, or read it to their child.

Books I Have Read

Name_____

	Title	Fiction/Nonfiction	Date
1.	_____	_____	_____
2.	_____	_____	_____
3.	_____	_____	_____
4.	_____	_____	_____
5.	_____	_____	_____
6.	_____	_____	_____
7.	_____	_____	_____
8.	_____	_____	_____
9.	_____	_____	_____
10.	_____	_____	_____
11.	_____	_____	_____
12.	_____	_____	_____
13.	_____	_____	_____
14.	_____	_____	_____
15.	_____	_____	_____
16.	_____	_____	_____
17.	_____	_____	_____
18.	_____	_____	_____

Balancing Literacy • K–2 © 2002 Creative Teaching Press

Parent-Child Reading Conference Form

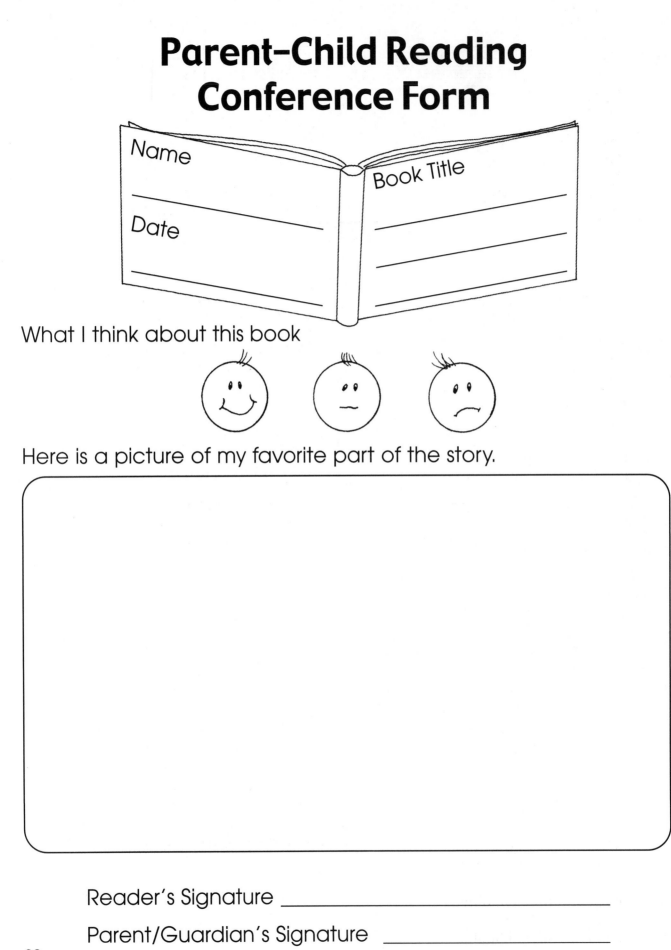

Name

Date

Book Title

What I think about this book

Here is a picture of my favorite part of the story.

Reader's Signature _____

Parent/Guardian's Signature _____

Balancing Literacy • K–2 © 2002 Creative Teaching Press

Bookmarks

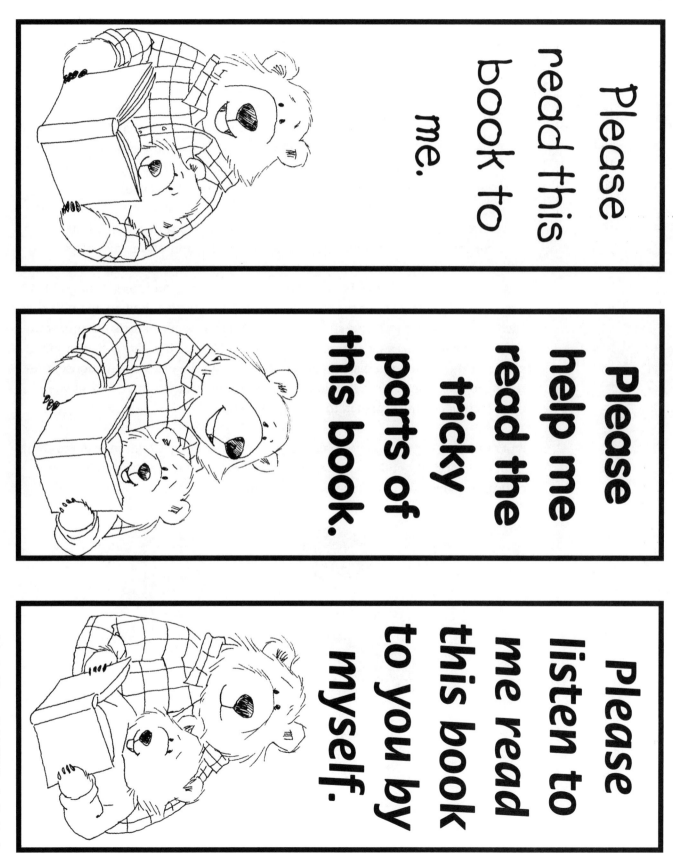

Please read this book to me.

Please help me read the tricky parts of this book.

Please listen to me read this book to you by myself.

Story Circles

Although it is beneficial to group children for guided reading sessions according to their current ability and use, it is also beneficial to allow children some freedom in small-group practice through self-selection and discussion of literature. One way to scaffold this process is by introducing Story Circles. Story Circles are the precursor to literature circles (which are usually developed by the end of second grade). Children must first participate in teacher-mediated, highly supported, small, self-selected groups to be prepared for literature circle participation.

Story Circles are small, temporary discussion groups comprised of children who have chosen to read the same story, poem, or book. After an initial introduction to Story Circles, the teacher may invite each group to read different books. (Most first- and second-grade teachers find that three to four groups are manageable.) Group members talk about the story together. Then, three members (who may each select an assistant) have specialized roles. The teacher models the procedures at first but later acts as facilitator for the groups. The teacher also collects multiple copies of the stories, poems, and books from which the groups can choose; pre-reads the selections before distributing them to the groups; and creates two or three lead questions designed to prompt "book talk."

Story Circles pave the way for children to become literate. Children begin to think "into the story" about the author's purpose and "beyond the story" to develop critical thinking and to attach personal meaning to the story.

Student Roles during Story Circle

There are three main student roles during Story Circle. The following are descriptions of these roles. Each leader may select an assistant so other children will be involved too.

The Talkmeister

Give this leader the discussion prompts, and ask him or her to initiate the group discussion. (After children are comfortable with the Story Circle format, invite them to create their own discussion prompts.) Use the directions on page 102 to create  a "Talkmeister Talking Stick" (a circle management tool) for each group. Have the Talkmeister ask a group member a question and then turn the talking stick upright. After the contents of the talking stick filter down to the bottom (this represents "think time"), the group member shares his or her answer. Ask the Talkmeister to repeat this process with other discussion questions.

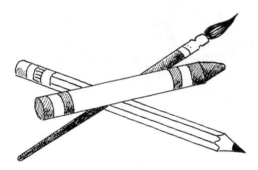

The Depictor

Ask the Depictor to draw, color, or paint an illustration that depicts the text the group reads. Ask the Depictor and his or her assistant to illustrate the characters, the setting, the beginning or ending of the story, or a favorite part. Have the leader draw the illustrations on the Story Flower Power reproducible (page 103).

The Fab Vocab-er

Ask this leader to listen for funny, hard, new, or interesting words from each day's reading. Make the Fab Vocab-er several copies of the Memory Tickets reproducible (page 104), and cut them apart. Decorate a bag, and write *Fab Vocab Bag* on it. Invite the Fab Vocab-er to write each word on a separate memory ticket and draw a corresponding picture. Place the completed tickets in the Fab Vocab Bag, and invite the whole class to review them.

Introducing Story Circles

When introducing Story Circles, provide plenty of modeling and guidance. Be sure children understand what your expectations are. Move slowly at first until all children understand the process, and then add a new role. The following schedule provides one way to gradually introduce Story Circles and may take several weeks to develop. Introduce each step and give children time to practice it for several days before introducing the next part of the process.

Step 1

Introduce the term "Story Circle" to the class. Explain that a Story Circle is a circle of children who get together to talk about good stories, books, and poems that they enjoy reading as a group. Select a short story or a Big Book, and read it to the class. (Have children sit in a large circle on the floor.) Ask one or two questions about the story, and invite children to comment on, ask questions about, and discuss the story.

Step 2

Hold up a talking stick (a rainstick). Explain that the Talkmeister leads the group's discussion and that anyone who wishes to speak must be holding the talking stick. Be sure children understand that a Story Circle is really a listening circle as well, and remind them how to listen to the person speaking without interrupting. Hold the talking stick upright, and share something about the story. Then, pass the stick to a child. Have that child hold the talking stick and say something about the story. Continue the process around the circle. Tell children that they may say *Pass* if they do not wish to speak.

The main characters were the dad, boy, and farmer.

Step 3

Introduce the role of the Depictor. Talk about how the Depictor responds to the story with a drawing or graphic rather than with words. Read aloud another short story or Big Book. Then, give each child a Story Flower Power reproducible (page 103). Have children draw in response to the story.

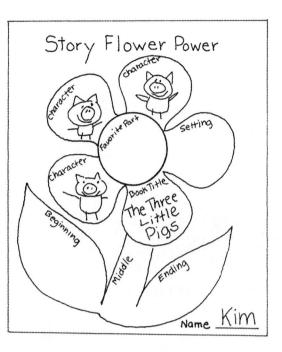

Step 4

Explain that the role of the Fab Vocab-er is to develop a fabulous vocabulary and help others do the same. Read aloud another short story or a poem (one with beautiful, vivid imagery or funny words). Give each child several copies of the Memory Tickets reproducible (page 104). Have children select words that are funny, interesting, or new to them. Help children correctly spell the words, and then invite them to sketch a picture that will help them remember each word. Place the completed tickets in the class Fab Vocab Bag, and invite children to review them at another time.

Talkmeister's Talking Stick

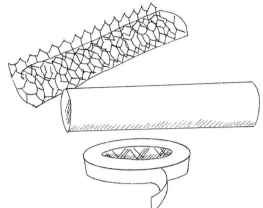

Materials
chicken wire (teacher use only)
empty paper-towel tube
masking tape
grains of rice, popcorn, and/or small pebbles
glue
butcher paper
art supplies or paint/paintbrush

1. Carefully coil the chicken wire, and slide it into the paper towel tube.

2. Seal one end of the tube with masking tape.

3. Place rice, popcorn and/or pebbles into the tube, and seal the other end.

4. Glue a piece of butcher paper around the tube so it is completely covered.

5. Decorate or paint the tube. Allow the tube to completely seal and dry before children use it.

6. Make a copy of the Talkmeister label. Cut out the label, and glue it on the tube.

Talkmeister

Balancing Literacy • K–2 © 2002 Creative Teaching Press

Story Flower Power

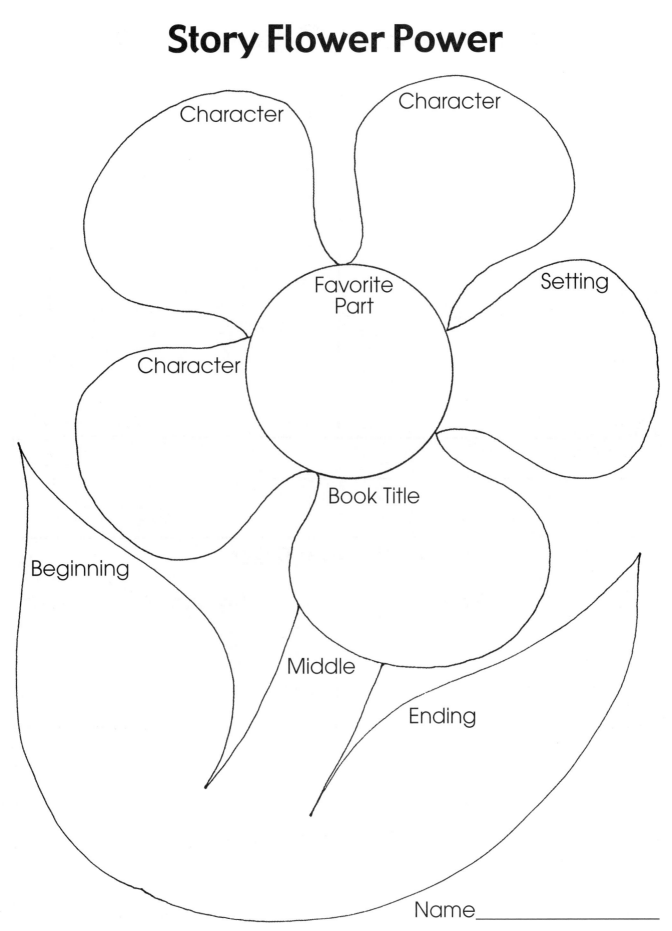

Character

Character

Setting

Favorite Part

Character

Book Title

Beginning

Middle

Ending

Name_____

Memory Tickets

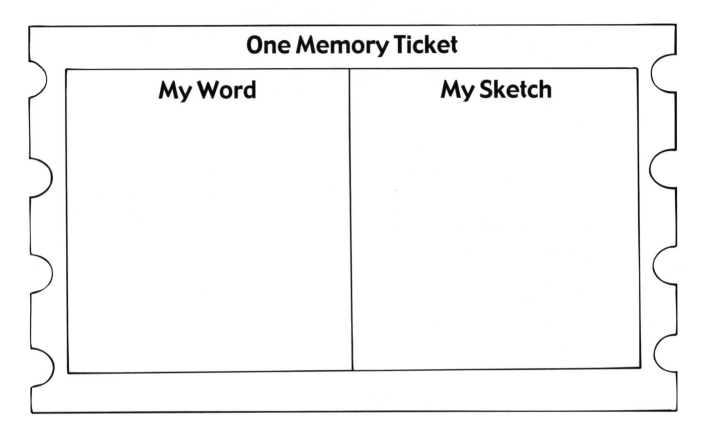

One Memory Ticket

My Word	My Sketch

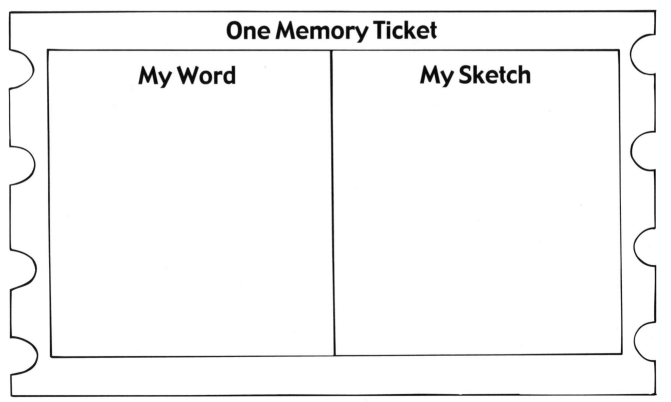

One Memory Ticket

My Word	My Sketch

Balancing Literacy • K–2 © 2002 Creative Teaching Press

Literacy Centers

Literacy centers provide an opportunity for all children to engage in meaningful literacy activities that enrich their skill development and understanding while allowing the teacher time to work with small groups or individuals. Literacy centers provide children with ample opportunities to read, write, speak, and listen; reinforce your existing reading/language arts program; accommodate different learning styles; and build children's self-esteem as they experience success.

Maximize your ability to organize materials and move children throughout the room by creating four main center areas: Reading Area, Writing and Illustrating Area, Spelling and Word Work Area, and Listening Post Area. Each area can contain several centers. These centers will evolve from your whole-group, small-group, and individual activities. For example, after reading a Big Book, place it in the Big Book Center, or after singing a song, place the taped version in the Poem and Song Center. This method of center development allows you to have center materials that children already know how to use. As a result, you will have more time to work uninterrupted with small groups or individuals.

Have an open area for whole-group reading, creation of wall stories, dramatization, and music and movement. Arrange materials in cabinets or on shelves so children can easily remove the materials and work with them on the floor or at a table. If you have limited storage space, use boxes, cans, folders, envelopes, and resealable plastic bags to create portable centers. Create matching labels or use matching stickers to identify each material and the shelf on which it is stored so children will know where to pick up and return center materials.

This section includes descriptions of the types of literacy centers to place in each area and ways to manage your centers.

Managing Your Centers

Slowly introduce literacy centers throughout the first few weeks of school. Start out by having the whole class participate in each center until children understand what they are to do at it. Train children not to interrupt you during center time. Children should be able to work independently at centers. The optimum management is self-management in which children self-select their centers, complete the center activity, and clean up at the end of center time. However, this does not happen overnight. Initially, you may choose to create a system to help with center movement. Below are two methods of rotating children in centers.

Rotating Wheel

Divide the class into four groups. Cut a "wheel" (circle) out of poster board, and divide it into four sections. Write the names of the children in each group in a separate section. Divide a large piece of poster board into four sections, and label each section with the name of a center area. Use a brass fastener to attach the wheel to the poster board. Invite children to check the wheel to see which center area they will work in. Rotate the wheel each day for four days. (Groups will visit a different center area each day.) Give children a special project on Friday, or allow them to visit the center area of their choice.

Pocket Chart

Write the name of each center area on a separate index card or sentence strip. Draw a picture to represent each area. Place the cards or strips in a pocket chart. Create a name card for each child. Have children place their name card in the pocket chart under the center area they want to work at that day.

Remember to introduce and model each center activity before putting it in a center area. Nothing should be new to children. Each week, give each child a My Center Time Record reproducible (page 115). Have children identify what they did at each center and how they felt about their work each day at the end of center time. Collect and review the completed forms to keep track of which centers children participate in and how they felt about each one.

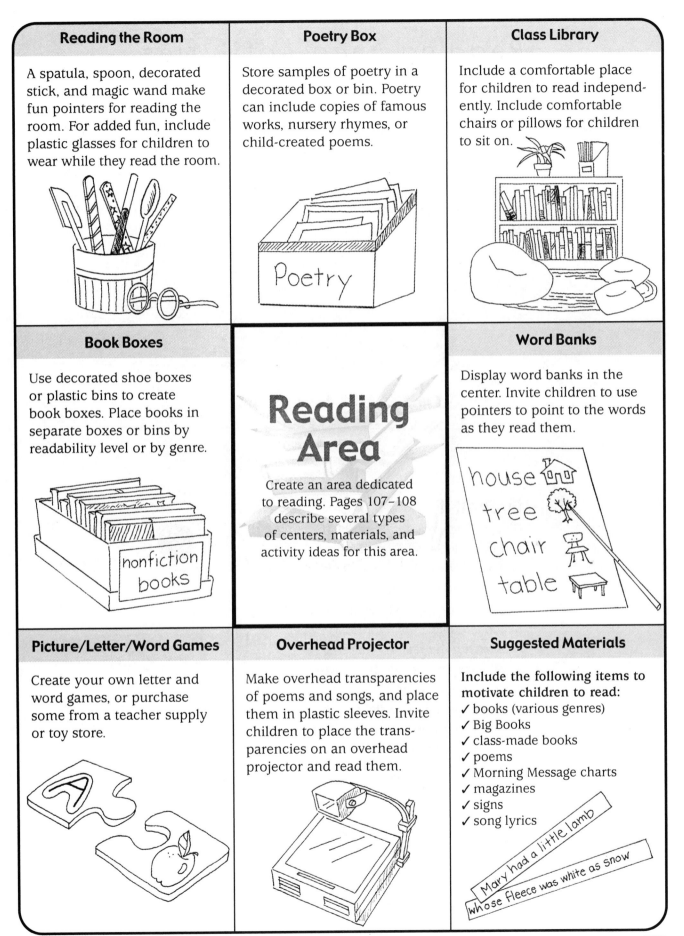

Reading the Room

A spatula, spoon, decorated stick, and magic wand make fun pointers for reading the room. For added fun, include plastic glasses for children to wear while they read the room.

Poetry Box

Store samples of poetry in a decorated box or bin. Poetry can include copies of famous works, nursery rhymes, or child-created poems.

Class Library

Include a comfortable place for children to read independently. Include comfortable chairs or pillows for children to sit on.

Book Boxes

Use decorated shoe boxes or plastic bins to create book boxes. Place books in separate boxes or bins by readability level or by genre.

Reading Area

Create an area dedicated to reading. Pages 107–108 describe several types of centers, materials, and activity ideas for this area.

Word Banks

Display word banks in the center. Invite children to use pointers to point to the words as they read them.

Picture/Letter/Word Games

Create your own letter and word games, or purchase some from a teacher supply or toy store.

Overhead Projector

Make overhead transparencies of poems and songs, and place them in plastic sleeves. Invite children to place the transparencies on an overhead projector and read them.

Suggested Materials

Include the following items to motivate children to read:
✓ books (various genres)
✓ Big Books
✓ class-made books
✓ poems
✓ Morning Message charts
✓ magazines
✓ signs
✓ song lyrics

Reading Area Activities

Pocket Chart Activity

Write each line of a poem, song, or chant from a shared reading activity on a separate sentence strip. Place the same type of sticker on the back of each strip. Hole- punch each strip, and place the strips on a binder ring. Invite children to remove the strips from the ring and place them in the correct order in a pocket chart. Encourage children to use a pointer as they read and reread the sentence strips.

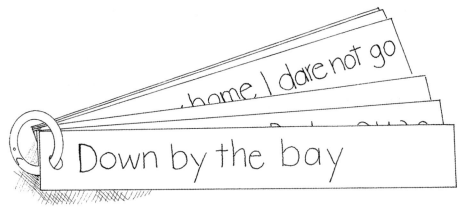

Eyeball It

Glue a wiggly eye to the tip of a craft stick. Select target letters and/or sight words from shared reading material. Write the target letters and/or sight words on chart paper, and place the chart at a center with the reading material, small sticky notes, and the wiggly-eye craft stick. Invite children to copy a target letter or sight word from the chart onto a small sticky note and attach the note on the wiggly-eye stick. Have children reread the reading material and use the stick as a pointer. Ask them to count how many times the target letter or word appears in the reading material.

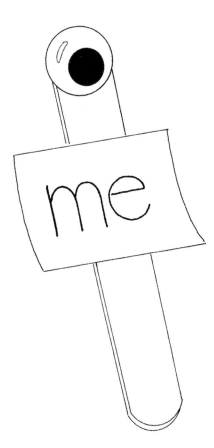

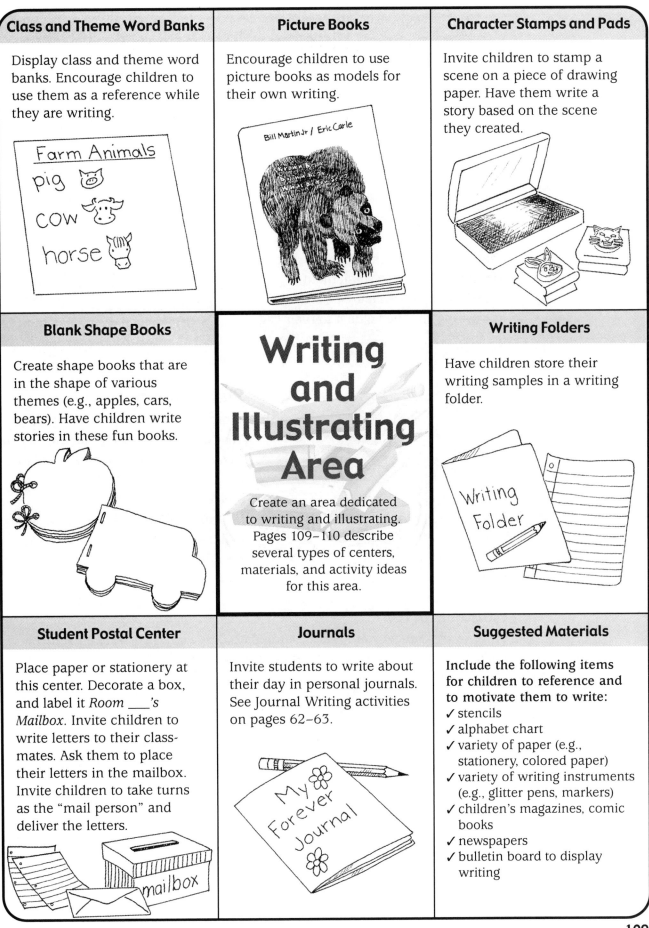

Class and Theme Word Banks

Display class and theme word banks. Encourage children to use them as a reference while they are writing.

Farm Animals
pig
cow
horse

Picture Books

Encourage children to use picture books as models for their own writing.

Bill Martin Jr / Eric Carle

Character Stamps and Pads

Invite children to stamp a scene on a piece of drawing paper. Have them write a story based on the scene they created.

Blank Shape Books

Create shape books that are in the shape of various themes (e.g., apples, cars, bears). Have children write stories in these fun books.

Writing and Illustrating Area

Create an area dedicated to writing and illustrating. Pages 109–110 describe several types of centers, materials, and activity ideas for this area.

Writing Folders

Have children store their writing samples in a writing folder.

Writing Folder

Student Postal Center

Place paper or stationery at this center. Decorate a box, and label it *Room ___'s Mailbox.* Invite children to write letters to their class-mates. Ask them to place their letters in the mailbox. Invite children to take turns as the "mail person" and deliver the letters.

mailbox

Journals

Invite students to write about their day in personal journals. See Journal Writing activities on pages 62–63.

My Forever Journal

Suggested Materials

Include the following items for children to reference and to motivate them to write:
✓ stencils
✓ alphabet chart
✓ variety of paper (e.g., stationery, colored paper)
✓ variety of writing instruments (e.g., glitter pens, markers)
✓ children's magazines, comic books
✓ newspapers
✓ bulletin board to display writing

Writing and Illustrating Area Activities

Peek-Through Bags

Gather a class set of paper lunch bags. Cut out a square on one side of each bag. Invite children to draw on the outside of the bag the setting of a story they would like to write. Then, ask them to draw one or two characters for their story on drawing paper. Have children cut out their characters and place them in the bag. Ask them to write a story about their characters and setting and then glue it to their bag (as shown).

Story Starter Sticks

Write story starter sentences (e.g., *The best thing that ever happened to me was . . .*) on separate craft sticks. Store the sticks in a can labeled *Story Starters,* and place the can in the Writing and Illustrating Area. Invite children to take a stick whenever they need help with a story idea.

Rebus Stories

Place several rubber stamps and stamp pads in the writing center area. Invite children to use the stamps to create a rebus story.

Typewriters	Computers and Software	Picture/Word File
Invite children to practice spelling words by typing them on a typewriter.	Have children work with computer software that provides spelling practice.	Cut out magazine pictures. Glue each picture on a separate index card, and label each card. For example, write *dog* underneath the picture of a dog. Store the cards alphabetically in a box.

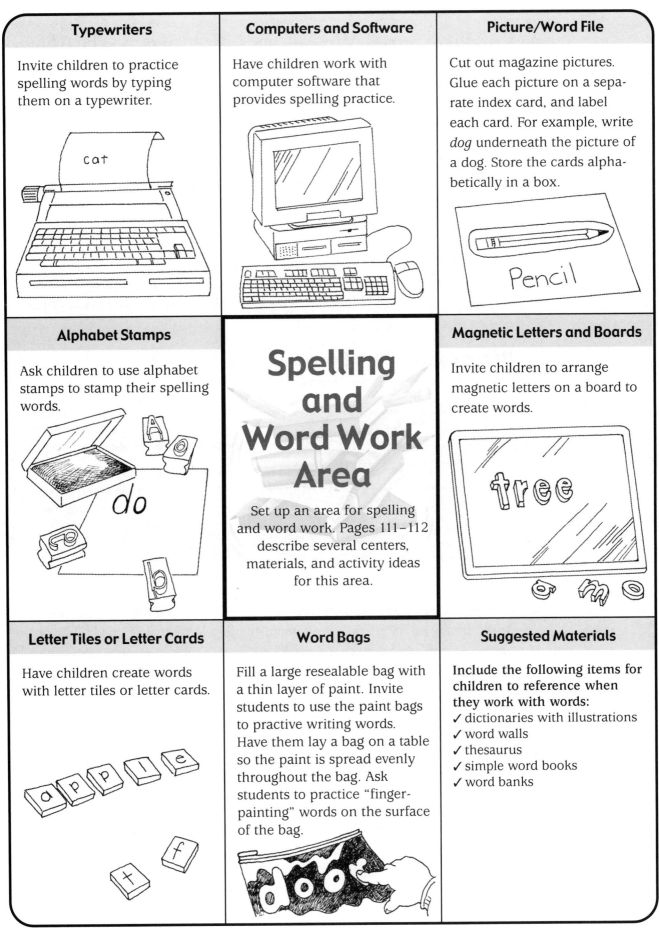

Alphabet Stamps

Ask children to use alphabet stamps to stamp their spelling words.

Spelling and Word Work Area

Set up an area for spelling and word work. Pages 111–112 describe several centers, materials, and activity ideas for this area.

Magnetic Letters and Boards

Invite children to arrange magnetic letters on a board to create words.

Letter Tiles or Letter Cards

Have children create words with letter tiles or letter cards.

Word Bags

Fill a large resealable bag with a thin layer of paint. Invite students to use the paint bags to practive writing words. Have them lay a bag on a table so the paint is spread evenly throughout the bag. Ask students to practice "finger-painting" words on the surface of the bag.

Suggested Materials

Include the following items for children to reference when they work with words:
✓ dictionaries with illustrations
✓ word walls
✓ thesaurus
✓ simple word books
✓ word banks

Spelling and Word Work Area Activities

Sound Puzzles

Cut die-cut shapes into parts to represent the number of sounds in the word. For example, cut a pig die cut into three parts and a cow die cut into two parts. Write the letters that represent each sound on the corresponding piece. Place the pieces of each shape into a separate resealable plastic bag, and store the bags in the Spelling and Word Work Area. Invite children to assemble the "puzzles." Encourage them to slowly take apart a puzzle, say each sound in the word, and blend the sounds as they put the pieces back together.

Word Family Step Books

Select a target rime. Create step books using the following directions:

- For each book, stack three sheets of drawing paper and pull up each sheet a short distance so the bottom edges are visible.

- Fold the three sheets of paper over, bringing the top down to the bottom and staggering a small piece of each sheet to create a six-step book.

- Fold a construction paper cover over the sheets, leaving a portion of the first page showing.

- Use a stapler to bind the book.

Place blank step books and crayons or markers in the Spelling and Word Work Area. Identify the target rime, and invite children to write a word-family word on the portion of each page that sticks out. Have children write on the hidden portion a phrase or sentence that includes the word and/or add an illustration.

Snap to It!

Select target rimes. Use a permanent marker to write the vowels for the rimes on yellow linking cubes, one vowel per cube. Write the ending consonant(s) of the rimes on red linking cubes. Link yellow and red cubes to create your target rimes. Write each consonant on a separate green cube, and place the green linking cubes in a box. Place the cubes and writing paper in the Spelling and Word Work Area. Invite children to attach green onset cubes to the yellow and red cubes to create words. Have them list the word-family words, real or nonsense, on writing paper and circle the real words.

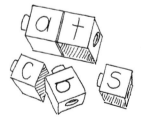

Cassette Recorders/CD Players

Invite children to listen to books on cassettes or CDs.

Individual Cassette Players

Ask parents to lend individual cassette players and headphones for the class to use during the school year.

Read–Aloud Session

Tape-record yourself as you read aloud a book to the class. Also, record the class discussion of the story. Store the cassette and read-aloud book in a large resealable plastic bag.

Personal Student Cassettes

Have children tape-record themselves reading stories they wrote. Place each author's story and cassette in a separate resealable plastic bag. Place the bags, a cassette player, and headphones in a listening center. Invite children to listen to a classmate's recording as they read his or her story.

Listening Post Area

Set up an area for listening to stories and music. Pages 113–114 describe several types of centers, materials, and activity ideas for this area.

Class-Made Story Cassettes

Tape-record the class reading a class-made book. Store the book and cassette in a resealable plastic bag.

Thematic Poems

Make copies of poems from shared or guided reading activities. Tape-record a volunteer reading the poem, and store the poem and cassette in a resealable plastic bag.

Songs and Lyrics

Write the lyrics to songs children have sung in class. Store the recorded version of the songs and the written lyrics in separate resealable plastic bags.

Classical Music

Invite children to listen to classical music.

Listening Post Area Activities

Name That Sound

Tape-record common sounds (e.g., dog barking, door closing, ball bouncing). Cut out a magazine picture that corresponds to each recorded sound. Mount each picture on construction paper, and laminate the papers for durability. Place the cassette and pictures in a resealable plastic bag. Invite children to listen to the cassette and find the picture that matches each sound.

Introducing Interviews

Have children brainstorm interview questions. Ask them to use their questions to interview a classmate, family member, or school staff member. Have children tape-record their interviews. Store each child's cassette and interview questions in a separate resealable plastic bag. Invite children to listen to the interviews and read the questions.

I Like What I Heard

Make several copies of the Listening Post reproducible (page 116), and place them in your Listening Post Area. Invite children to complete the form each time they listen to a recording of a book. Encourage fluent writers to write a sentence about their favorite part of the recording.

My Center Time Record

Name _____

Draw a picture of what you did during center time each day.
Indicate how you felt about each center.

	M	T	W	TH	F
Reading Area					
Writing and Illustrating Area					
Spelling and Word Work Area					
Listening Post Area					

Listening Post

Name _____   Date _____

Title _____

Author _____

I thought this book was

Great

Okay

Yucky

Here is a picture of my favorite part.

Balancing Literacy • K–2 © 2002 Creative Teaching Press

Assessment

Assessment is an ongoing process throughout the year. Use assessment and evaluations to guide your classroom instruction and to meet the needs of the children.

There is an endless number of ways to assess children: tests, observations, checklists, rubrics, and interviews are just a few. Knowing what information you want to get will help you choose the types of assessment to use.

This section provides various assessment methods and strategies, including ways to assess your children's progress in reading, writing, spelling, and phonics. Choose the reproducibles that best meet your specific assessment needs. Or, use them as springboards to creating your own meaningful assessment tools.

Types of Assessment

There are several ways to assess children. The following explains some of the different forms of assessment.

Authentic Assessment occurs when children read real text, write about meaningful topics, discuss books, keep journals, write letters, and revise their own writing. There are two types of authentic assessment: performance assessment and ongoing assessment.

Performance assessment is when children demonstrate their knowledge, skills, and strategies by creating a response such as a report, draw and write about a story, or read aloud a section of a story.

Ongoing assessment is based on more than just one sample of a child's work and abilities. Instead, the teacher keeps a portfolio of each child's work samples throughout the school year. These samples can be chosen by the teacher and/or the child. When children choose the work sample, have them complete a For My Portfolio reproducible (page 119) to explain why they chose that work. Include your comments, and invite parents to review their child's work and add their own comments on the form too. Attach the completed form to the work sample, and place it in the child's portfolio.

Informal Assessment includes making observations and recording those observations on checklists or anecdotal records. Make several copies of the Anecdotal Records reproducible (page 120), and keep them on a clipboard. Carry the clipboard with you while you observe children, and make notes about each child. Cut apart the anecdotal records, and place them in the appropriate child's portfolio. For each child, copy the Writing Assessment Checklist reproducible (page 121) and the Oral Reading Record reproducible (page 122). Use these forms to assess children's writing and reading skills.

Student Self-assessment occurs when children assess their own work. This form of assessment helps children compare their work over time, set personal goals, and evaluate their own progress.

For My Portfolio

Name _____   Date_____

Student Comments

I chose this work because _____

_____

_____

_____

_____

Parent Comments

_____

_____

_____

_____

_____

Teacher Comments

_____

_____

_____

_____

_____

Balancing Literacy • *K–2* © 2002 Creative Teaching Press

Anecdotal Records

Name _____   Date _____

Reading Behaviors

Writing Behaviors

Center Behaviors

Name _____   Date _____

Reading Behaviors

Writing Behaviors

Center Behaviors

Name _____   Date _____

Reading Behaviors

Writing Behaviors

Center Behaviors

Writing Assessment Checklist

Name _____   Date _____

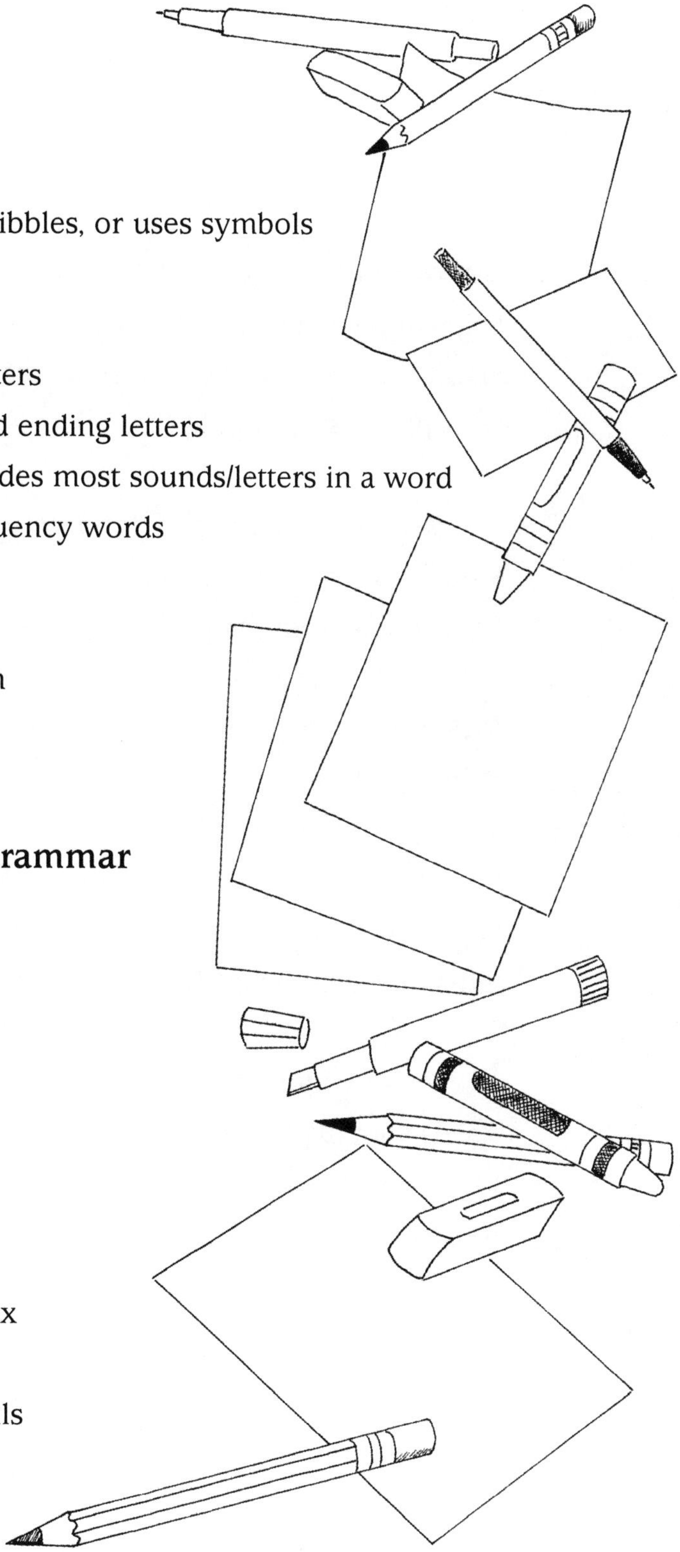

Writing Mechanics

_____ Uses a picture to write

_____ Writes in letter strings, scribbles, or uses symbols

_____ Writes left to right

_____ Writes random letters

_____ Uses mostly beginning letters

_____ Uses mostly beginning and ending letters

_____ Writes by sound and includes most sounds/letters in a word

_____ Correctly writes high-frequency words

_____ Uses correct spacing

_____ Uses capital letters

_____ Correctly uses punctuation

Writing Process and Grammar

_____ Chooses own topic

_____ Reads writing to others

_____ Uses simple beginning

_____ Uses simple middle

_____ Uses simple ending

_____ Sequences ideas

_____ Uses descriptive words

_____ Uses sentence structure

   ❑ simple   ❑ complex

_____ Writes dialogue

_____ Uses beginning editing skills

Oral Reading Record

Name _____   Teacher _____

Book Selected By _____   Date _____

Book Title _____

check all
that apply

Reading Strategies Observed

_____ Skips unknown word and reads on

_____ Starts over and reads whole sentence

_____ Uses phonics knowledge as a clue (sounds out part or all of word)

_____ Uses picture as a clue

_____ Guesses what the word might be

_____ Stops reading, won't go on

_____ Stops but asks for help

Miscues

_____ Skips words

_____ Inserts words

_____ Self-corrects miscues so text makes sense

_____ Says incorrect word but keeps intended meaning (e.g., says *dog,* but word is *puppy*)

_____ Substitutes phonetically similar words (e.g., replaces *this* with *that*)

Comprehension

_____ Reads with expression

_____ Identifies main character, setting, and story problem

_____ Retells the story

Balancing Literacy • K–2 © 2002 Creative Teaching Press

English–Language Learners

Many teachers are currently faced with the opportunity and challenge of working with children who are coming to know English as their second language. These learners vary in background experiences and in English-speaking ability. The following section describes the stages of English-language learning and presents fun, meaningful ways in which to engage your English-language learners (E.L.L.) and help them succeed as readers and writers.

Use the teaching strategies and activities (pages 125–126) and games (pages 127–128) to meet the needs of your E.L.L. students. Include all of your children in the classroom routine to make them feel like they are a part of the learning community. But remember, feeling a part of a new situation does not happen overnight; it takes time and patience on the part of you and the other children

Stages of English-Language Learning

The following stages represent a broad continuum of language proficiency from little or no experience with English to nearly native fluency with the language. It is important to understand these stages so you can target where your children are and how you can help them. The following describes characteristics of children at each stage:

Preproduction Stage (The Silent Period)

- Usually new to the United States
- Do not have basic vocabulary
- Often cannot ask for help
- May appear to be withdrawn
- Cannot get basic needs met through language

Early Speech Production Stage

- Beginning to follow basic grammar patterns of English
- Have a limited but growing vocabulary
- Tend to speak in one- or two-word sentences
- Often do not feel comfortable enough to initiate or to extend conversations

Speech Emergence Stage

- Are beginning to produce language with fewer misunderstandings
- Demonstrate growing independence with language
- Are developing a good sight word vocabulary
- Often still have trouble when asked to develop ideas or expand upon a thought or statement

Intermediate Fluency Stage

- Speak English with ease
- Feel comfortable switching back and forth between first and second languages
- Are comfortable initiating conversations
- May still have problems with complex pronunciation and grammar
- Are improving daily through seeing and hearing others around them use language

Use these classroom-tested strategies and activities to meet the needs of your English-language learners.

Buddy Up

Assign a buddy to each English-language learner. Choose children who know the school and routine well and, if possible, can speak the child's native language. Ask the buddy to help the other child throughout the day but not complete all the tasks for the child.

One More Time

Slow your speaking rate. Also make an effort to simplify your language, shorten your sentences, and clearly pronounce words. Repeat and emphasize key words. Use fewer pronouns and contractions, and avoid idioms.

Show Me

Clarify your words by pointing to pictures and props, drawing simple sketches, and using gestures, facial expressions, and body language.

Yes or No

During small-group work, assign E.L.L. children tasks that require little or no language, such as painting or drawing. Gradually increase their level of participation by having them point, draw, or perform an appropriate action. When incorporating verbal responses, ask questions that require only a yes or no answer or a one-word response. For responses that require more speech, have children sit with a buddy for collaboration and support.

Rhythm, Rhyme, and Repetition

Provide a print-rich environment with materials that involve rhyme, repetition, and predictability.

Sing It to Learn It

Teach concepts and language through music. Sing about the concepts you want children to learn. Children will memorize the concepts as they develop knowledge of the language.

Back to Basics

Teach "basic needs" vocabulary and processes first. For example, teaching words for body parts will enable children to begin to respond to physical commands.

You're Cool, I'm Cool

Demonstrate respect for each child's first language and native culture. Try to label certain classroom objects in the first language of E.L.L. children as well as in English. Use a different color label for each language.

Q & A Time

Have children practice high-frequency sentence patterns by asking a series of children the same open-ended question following familiar story patterns. Use the following examples as a model:

(name), (name), what do you see? I see a <u>ball</u> in front of me.

(name), (name), what do you see? I see a <u>doll</u> in front of me.

Encore

Provide opportunities for children to repeat activities and games introduced during whole-group lessons. Place the materials in learning center areas. Have English-language learners work in small groups or with a buddy to review the activity or game.

Listen Up

Tape-record all songs and rhymes introduced during whole-group lessons on cassettes. Place the cassettes and copies of the songs and rhymes in the Listening Post Area. Encourage E.L.L. children to listen to the recordings and repeat the songs and rhymes. Invite them to clap or tap along with chants. Add gestures to songs and rhymes to reinforce the rhythm, intonation, and stress of the language.

Have children practice English by playing these delightful games with them.

Pass the Ball

1 Have children sit in a circle on the floor. Ask children to pass a ball around the circle. As they are passing the ball, have them sing the following chant:

> *I'll pass the ball from me to you. I'll pass the ball to you.*
> *I'll pass the ball from me to you. I'll pass the ball to you.*

2 Gradually add names or descriptive words or change objects to add to their vocabulary development. For example, have children sing *I'll pass the yellow ball from me to you. I'll pass the ball to you* or *I'll pass the small yellow ball from me to you. I'll pass the ball to you.*

I'll pass the ball from me to you. I'll pass the ball to you.

Mary Wore Her Red Dress

1 Read aloud *Mary Wore Her Red Dress and Henry Wore his Green Sneakers* by Merle Peek (Houghton Mifflin).

2 Sing the song from the book with the class.

3 Have children create a class book based on the text pattern. Encourage children to replace words from the song with classmates' names, items of clothing, and colors to create a text innovation. For example, children may change the sentence *Mary wore her red dress all day long* to *Alex wore his blue shorts all day long.*

Act It Out

1. Write five basic verbs (e.g., *run, hop, smile, clap, hug*) on separate pieces of construction paper.

2. Choose one word to talk about each day of the week. Dramatize the word for the class.

3. Have a child illustrate the word on the construction paper.

4. Mix up the "action verb cards," and place them facedown in a pile. Ask a pair of children to select one action verb card. Encourage them to silently act out the word for the class without showing the picture.

5. Invite the rest of the class to identify which verb the pair is dramatizing.

Concentrate on My Feelings

1. Draw faces that reflect various emotions (e.g., happy, sad, angry, surprised) on separate paper plates.

2. Draw or cut out from a magazine a scene that reflects each emotion, and glue each picture to a paper plate.

3. Place the two sets of plates in a learning center, and invite children to use the plates to play Memory.

4. Ask children to place all the paper plates facedown and take turns turning over two plates at a time. When children pick two plates that match (emotion face with the corresponding emotion scene), ask them to dramatize the emotion and state the way they are feeling. For example, a child who matches the "happy" plates might say *I feel happy*. Later, have children extend the activity to describe the scene on the plate. For example, they might say *I feel happy when I eat birthday cake*.